When the Fire

goes out

When the Fire goes out

A Journey to the Spirit World

Otto Matthias

Order this book online at www.trafford.com
or email orders@trafford.com

Most Trafford titles are also available at major online book retailers.

Printed in Victoria, BC, Canada.

ISBN: 978-1-4269-3190-1 (sc)
ISBN: 978-1-4269-3191-8 (hc)
ISBN: 978-1-4269-3192-5 (eb)

Library of Congress Control Number: 2010906118

Our mission is to efficiently provide the world's finest, most comprehensive book publishing service, enabling every author to experience success. To find out how to publish your book, your way, and have it available worldwide, visit us online at www.trafford.com

Trafford rev. 05/14/2010

 www.trafford.com

North America & international
toll-free: 1 888 232 4444 (USA & Canada)
phone: 250 383 6864 ♦ fax: 812 355 4082

Table of Contents

Introduction

How do you communicate a revelation, a paradigm shift, akin to a devout priest tugging at a loose corner on the back cover of his bible and finding therein a series of pages with a hidden gospel that flies in the face of all he believed was true? I sought such an experience and found it, and discovered that the unknown was not as I expected.

My life had been a comfortable one. Never had my existence or sanity been truly threatened, neither by poverty nor menace. This good fortune, however, left me naive, soft and bored, and eager to explore the dark edges of the world.

As a child I was fascinated with magic, ghosts, myths and monsters, and later my interests evolved into religion, philosophy and the occult. Human society and the physical world seemed to me fleeting shadows of something more substantial and more enduring; something that soaked through everything like a deep dark ocean through a sheet of paper. Architecture, myths, science and religions were like descriptions of wine without a taste of it. I needed a key to unlock the door of physical illusion. I found that door in my mind, and the key was an altered state of consciousness.

My first revelation came when I tried magic mushrooms at age nineteen. I had a mystical experience and recognized that we were all extensions of a single energy, interfacing with physical reality through ephemeral bodies. It was wondrous and liberating, but it failed to take me behind the curtain. I wanted to transcend mundane reality and understand its underpinnings, and came to believe that this holy grail would be found in an Ayahuasca ceremony.

The word Ayahuasca means vine of the soul or vine of the dead, and it is at once the name of a vine and the psychedelic brew of which it is the primary ingredient. Since time immemorial, Amazonian natives have used Ayahuasca to heal and to learn. They say that it opens a door to the spirit world.

I continued about my life doing what was necessary, all the while searching and longing to see beyond the veil of my hamster wheel. When I was 31 I dropped everything and backpacked through India for five months, however only to return to my previous grind. I found solace in the certainty that eventually my life would end and death would release me from my bonds. Then came the day, when I was 34 and feeling especially frustrated, that I decided: "That's it! I'm going to the Amazon!"

The journey is its own reward

Vancouver to Houston

My journey began on a typical winter morning in Vancouver, Canada. It was dark, dingy, cold and wet. Natalia, the woman who lived across the hall and who I reluctantly embraced as my girlfriend, had offered to drive Andrei and me to the airport at 5am. Andrei was a colleague from work who lived nearby. Groggily captivated by rain drops rolling down the windshield, Natalia and I sat in her Honda Civic and waited outside Andrei's apartment building. He was late. He had partied the night through and was only now stuffing clothes into his bags.

Andrei was not accompanying me to the Amazon. In fact, none of my friends had been willing to join me. He was merely sharing my flight to Houston and from there he would fly to Mexico while I continued to Peru.

Andrei emerged from the building and climbed into the back seat. The trip to the airport was a blur. I kissed

Natalia good-bye, filled out redundant forms and was fingerprinted and retina scanned at American customs like a criminal. Andrei and I walked to the terminal, boarded the plane and claimed the non-reclining seats at the very back next to the toilets.

I stared out the window and watched the rain turn to dribbling slush. "I will not miss this city," I thought. Although the weather report for Iquitos—my destination at the edge of the Amazon—called for ten days of thunderstorms, at least I would be warm. I had prepared by packing a poncho, scotchgarding my luggage and sealing valuables, including money, travelers checks, two cell phones, a diary and toilet paper, in zip-lock bags.

"You seem to be taking the delay rather well," said a perky stewardess with a pointy nose, a mop of red hair and a charming Tennessee accent. "Do you work for the airlines?"

"No, I don't," I replied. The plane remained grounded for two and a half hours while waiting to be hosed down with anti-freeze. I didn't mind, though, because I was back in the stream of life. Like an assembly line worker going to the bathroom, I had stepped out of the numbing groove of routine.

At long last, salmon colored antifreeze streamed over the windows. It looked like watered-down blood and we mused that a chicken had been sacrificed on the roof to appease the gods. The engines came to life, fresh air flowed through the cabin and soon we took off on an uneventful flight to Houston. I missed my connecting flight by thirty minutes, but Andrei was able to catch his. We hugged good-bye and parted at the airport.

The airline put me up at a hotel for the night. I lugged my bags outside to the bus stop and took up a strategic position next to a pretty girl. Although I knew the answer, I asked her if that was where the shuttle stopped. We got into a conversation and I found out that she had missed a connecting flight to the Bahamas where she was to meet her boyfriend.

The shuttle arrived, we grabbed seats at the back and continued talking. Her name was Julie, she had a degree in Psychology and practiced law in San Francisco. I told her that I also had a Psychology degree and that I was on my way to the Amazon to take Ayahuasca.

We walked into the hotel like a couple, got our rooms and agreed to meet in thirty minutes for dinner at the bar. I was exhausted from the flight. I cleaned my teeth, messed my hair and went downstairs. The bar was almost empty and I wondered if I was in the right place. Julie, who's name I had forgotten, was nowhere to be seen. I walked around and quibbled over where to sit. A table was a lonely place to wait while the bar offered little privacy and face to face contact. Eventually I settled on a stool at the corner of the bar, ordered a gin tonic and read the one page menu over and over.

After a few minutes Julie arrived and declared that she needed a glass of wine. We ordered food and discussed our respective relationships; both fairly new and uncertain. I moved to a pint of Sam Adams. I was attracted to Julie and felt like a mouse dancing on tables while the cat was away. We talked about ketamine, mushrooms, LSD, ecstasy and sexual adventures; clearly she was a kindred spirit. I wondered how far we would take it.

We paid up and stepped into the elevator. I felt that we could spend the night together but was too tipsy, tired and uncertain to pursue it. I assumed a passive and polite holding pattern. When the cabin arrived at my floor and the doors opened, we turned to each other and agreed that it was a pleasure to have met. We hugged and kissed good night. I returned to my room with a spring in my step, collapsed on the bed and sank into peaceful sleep.

Breakfast

"Ha-ha-ha, oh lord have mercy!" howled a buxom black waitress wearing a Santa hat as I walked into the dining room. When she saw me she asked "You wanna' half buffet or full buffet? You wan' hash browns 'n stuff?"

"Sure," I said.

"Okay shuga'!" She showed me to a table and brought a glass of orange juice. "There you go babe," she said.

I pulled out my diary and noted my regret at missing the full moon in the Amazon that night, when two waitresses broke into shrieks of laughter across the restaurant. I looked up and saw them talking to a man. The waitress in the Santa hat shouted at her friend "Now you see? He done started somethin'! Where you at?!"

I was fascinated by the waitresses and recorded their language. One might have accused them of being simple, fat and uneducated, but they were undeniably good natured. I thought of them later on as I sat next to a stern, square jawed pilot in a bomber jacket on the airport shuttle. For all his good looks and status, he was disagreeable and authoritative.

"Hey driver!" he called out, "Is this going to terminal B?"

"All Continental flights leave from E," replied the driver.

The pilot scowled and grumbled to himself: "That's not what my ticket says."

Back at breakfast, four old, white, prototypal suburban Americans, looking straight from the golf course, entered the restaurant and sat at a nearby table. They were regulars and the waitress treated them with accordant familiarity. They commented on her Santa hat and she cried out "You know what they tol' me, that one over there?!" She pointed to her colleague across the floor. "She said 'You ain't no angel,' an' I tol' her 'We all angels!'" Her ample bosom shook with laughter.

Houston to Lima

After breakfast I took the shuttle to the Houston airport. Throngs of people from all generations, cultures and classes came and went as I whiled away the hours at the terminal. It reminded me of time-lapse films of clouds billowing in and out of existence, or red and white car lights streaming across nighttime bridges.

An unkempt white guy sat down next to me. "Where you headed?" he asked.

"To Iquitos," I said, mispronouncing it ICKEY-toss when it should be i-KEY-toss.

"I'm going there too!" he declared. His hair was long and thin, his clothes sloppy and the skin around his lips was dry and flaky. He leaned in close and told me he was visiting a friend who had gotten married and opened an Internet café in Iquitos. "The bitch raped him," he said, "for his money, that is." I wasn't sure if he meant the wife or the city.

I happily lost the guy as I boarded the plane and sat next to a mannerly Indian couple named Jack and Nina. They lived in LA and traveled extensively. Together through the porthole window, we watched the sun set behind a cloud and cut its silhouette black against the orange sky.

I couldn't resist sharing that I was on my way to the Amazon to take Ayahuasca.

"That's an excellent idea," declared Jack to my surprise. "I've had profound hallucinations too!" Ten years ago, he said, he contracted a disease that peeled the skin from 80% of his body. He had to sleep on a special mattress that pumped a constant stream of air through perforations to keep his raw dermis from sticking to it. In this vulnerable state he acquired a secondary infection which caused severe hallucinations.

Unfortunately, Jack was not much of a story teller. I hoped for detailed accounts of fantastic dreamscapes, of fairy creatures and out of body experiences, but instead he sighed and claimed not to remember much. His single account was of a night when he was delusional, believed that he was to marry a stone and got up and got dressed for the ceremony.

"If you call that a profound hallucination," I thought, "then you haven't seen squat!" Getting up at night to prepare for imaginary visitors or prevent nonexistent alarms from going off was a regular thing for me. I didn't tell him that, however. His experience was a far cry from the spiritual entities and alien worlds that I hoped to contact in the Amazon.

Lima to Iquitos

It was past midnight when I entered the air conditioned lobby of the Lima airport. I went to a counter, added my name to the standby list for the 5am flight to Iquitos and lugged my bags upstairs to the Internet café to email Scott my arrival time.

Scott was the owner-operator of the Refugio Altiplano; the shamanic healing center at the destination of my journey. Two months earlier I had serendipitously found his site while bored at work and researching Ayahuasca. Based on good faith and web design alone, I had contacted Scott, booked the trip and left family and friends behind to spend Christmas in the Amazon. I cared about nothing else, and wanted to die on this adventure rather than bleed away my life as a wage slave in a cube farm.

After sending off emails and posting an update on my blog, I whiled away the remaining hours in a cluster seat in front of the check-in. With my bags between my feet, I watched the cleaning crew mop up the deserted terminal floor.

At 7:15am I landed in Iquitos, emerged from the plane and squinted into humid sunlight. My mind was a haze. I hadn't slept in a day and hadn't shaved in three. Carefully I walked down the airplane steps and crossed the wet tarmac toward a small building that served as shelter, baggage claim and waiting area. Half way there, I turned around and took a photo of the plane. Behind it, at the edge of the runway, was a wall of jungle with a dark column of smoke rising in the distance. To my left, in a knobby field of grass and shrubs, rusted the hulks of two retired airliners.

I entered the luggage shelter and was greeted by men with cardboard signs. The floor was concrete, and a conveyor belt cycled from inside the room to the outside through two openings in the wall. A man with a sign reading "Otto Mathers" came up to me and asked: "Refugio Altiplano?"

"Si-si," I replied.

He asked for my luggage tag and hurried off. Although the handlers heaved the bags onto the conveyor belt in plain view, the man rushed around, craned his neck and called out to the workers. He reminded me of my dog when he pretended not to know where the ball was. Before my bag could hit the belt he grabbed it, placed it triumphantly on a cart and wheeled it ten steps out the door to where a woman waited for me next to a sunbaked taxi.

The woman introduced herself as Mariela and said that she would take me to the Refugio. I reached down to pick up my bag but the man snatched it up, carried it a little closer to the car and then held out his hand expectantly. I realized then that the man was a porter, and not a helpful employee of the Refugio. I fished my chest pouch up through the neck of my shirt, pulled out $1 and handed it to him.

The man examined the bill carefully, held it up to the light and ran his fingers along the edges, and then handed it back with a rueful expression. Mariela explained that he wanted a bill that was less worn. "He should be happy with what I give him!" I thought, but I took the bill and exchanged it for one that was more crisp. Content with the state of the new bill, the man then complained that he wanted more. I looked at Mariela and asked what was customary. "Cinco! Cinco!" cried the man, but Mariela sighed and said "Tres." Reluctantly I gave the man two more dollars. I never requested his service and would happily have carried my own bag, but I was a stranger and dependent on the good will of the locals, and that had its price.

Mariela and I climbed into the cab and drove into a dusty landscape of crumbling architecture, billboards, blaring rickshaws and blue exhaust. It was depressing. I imagined how peaceful it would've been had the internal combustion engine never been invented, but then I could not have traveled to Peru this easily. It was a dilemma. The problem, however, was not technology, but the fact that the technology was not good enough. Had the vehicles been electric and fueled by solar energy, they would have been clean and quiet.

My spirits lifted as we came to a civilized plaza with flowerbeds and bleached walkways, and stopped in front of a garage door with a mandala painted on it. I got out and swayed feverishly in the sun as Mariela paid the driver. The garage had a dutch door—a door with two horizontal panels like those at a horse stable—built into the middle of it. Mariela removed three padlocks, opened the bottom half and climbed in. I ducked in after her, and entered a spacious, windowless room with sparse furniture and psychedelic art on the walls. The only illumination came from a patch of sun that beamed through the door onto the concrete floor.

A painting on the far wall caught my attention. It depicted huts in a jungle village, but their latticework extended up, beyond the familiar form, into enormous spaceship type structures. It represented to me a union of, or a bridge between, the tribal and the modern. I heard the rickshaws screaming in the street, and thought that our civilization was in an intermediary step between the two.

Mariela went to a blue canister at the back of the room and poured herself a glass of water. I thought it terribly rude that she did not offer me any, but was not about to ask for some because I did not trust its quality. I decided to hold out until the Refugio.

"You owe money," declared Mariela flatly, and I understood that she meant the second half of my payment for ten days at the Refugio. I opened the lock on my pack, retrieved $800 and handed it to her. "I will give you a receipt," she said, and never did. I didn't care. I was exhausted and dehydrated, and just wanted to get to where I was going.

The spotlight of my consciousness narrowed. We left the garage, locked the door and took another taxi to a nearby riverbank. Children crowded round and waved perspiring bottles of brightly colored liquid at me. I wished I could have had some, but their water was even less trustworthy than that in the blue canister. I stumbled down a flight of steps to a rickety pier, and climbed into a motorboat with wooden benches and a canvas top. Two men were already on board. Mariela got in behind me, the motor sprang to life with a cough of oily smoke and we pulled into the cocoa brown waters of the Amazon. Looking back I saw rusty boats and a muddy shoreline ravaged by a slum of jumbled shacks.

Into the Amazon

The riverbank changed from the rape of an impoverished culture to the impenetrable tangle of unruly vegetation. Although the weather was hot, I shivered in the wind. I put on a fleece and a windbreaker, and huddled my arms around me.

We passed a crude raft with children playing on it. They waved to us and we waved back, and I thought how much healthier it was for a child to play on a log under an open sky than to sit at a desk in a closed room. I closed my burning eyes and dozed off. The boat turned from one river into the next and branched ever deeper into the Amazon.

An hour must have gone by when the motor dropped to an idle and the air grew muggy. I opened my eyes and saw that the width of the river had contracted from a kilometer to less than 50 meters. Lush trees towered overhead. I pulled off my fleece and windbreaker as the boat coasted toward a dock. The dock, together with a staircase leading into the jungle, was the only man-made structure in sight. We landed, disembarked and climbed up the stairs. At the top we emerged into a clearing and were greeted by a group of native women sitting on a wooden platform. They waved and offered us pipes, walking sticks, jewelery and other ornaments.

Mariela called out: "Señor Otto ha llegado!"

"Welcome Otto, you finally made it! How are you feeling?" came the reply from a two story building a little way ahead of us. The structure consisted of a wooden frame, walls of chartreuse green mosquito netting and a pitched roof made of leaves. On the second floor was a balcony with a hammock.

"I'm thirsty!" I blurted out, and regretted my poor manners.

"Well, come on up!" he said.

I walked up to the porch and opened the rickety door. Inside was an open space with two support pillars, a straight staircase along the side and two kayaks and an outboard motor on the floor. I ascended the stairs and entered Scott's living area. There was a table next to each pillar: one piled high with books and the other crowded with bottles filled with mysterious brown liquid. There was a bed draped with a white mosquito net, a cabinet brimming with clothes, a dozen pairs of rubber- and cowboy boots against the wall, and a third table with all manner of ornaments, pipes, jewelery and other knick-knacks on it. Next to the mouth of the stairs was a seating area with two couches and a coffee table. On the table stood a tray with a jug of water and two glasses.

Scott came up and shook my hand. He was tall and slim with red hair, pink skin and a silvery beard. He looked about 50. He filled a glass with water and handed it to me. I downed it, asked for another and finished that too.

"Thank you," I said, and heaved a sigh of relief.

"Please, have a seat," he said. "How was your trip? Did you find everything okay?"

The cordial inquiry felt strangely out of place in that environment. "Never mind that," I thought, "tell me about Ayahuasca!" but I replied: "Everything was fine, thanks. This place is wonderful!"

"Thank you, we're proud of it," he said.

"So, are we going to do Ayahuasca tonight?" I asked. "Where do you do it? What is it like?" I was bursting with curiosity and wanted all my questions answered at once, but in my wound up and worn down state I could neither carry a conversation nor absorb the answers.

He studied me with an amused twinkle in his eye. "We might have a ceremony," he replied calmly. "It'll depend on how the others feel about it." Scott had an easy manner and generously fielded my questions, but I also felt a hard edge in him that was not to be trifled with. When I had settled down a bit he asked: "Are you hungry? Why don't I show you your room and then we can get some breakfast."

We left his house and walked down a path which quickly became so riddled with roots and covered with leaves, that I would lose sight of it at night. We passed two buildings of similar construction to Scott's and then, on a gentle mound at the bottom of the path, we came to a harmonious structure with two balconies and an enormous roof. It would be my home for the ensuing ten days. I could look straight through the mesh walls and see the jungle on the other side.

Scott opened the door and showed me into a large room with an uneven spiral staircase in the middle. On the far side was the door to the bathroom. The bathroom was the only room with solid walls, although there were gaps between the boards large enough to accommodate a small snake. Two large windows provided light by day, and by night I would need to use candles or a flashlight. Half the floor was concrete and the other half wood. The concrete side had a shower and a black toilet, and the wooden side had a mirror and a black sink. Scott explained that running water came from a tank on the roof.

We mounted the rustic steps to the second floor where the sun filled jungle glowed brilliantly through the mesh walls. The only furniture in the house had been arranged in a cozy alcove above the bathroom. There was a platform with a simple mattress on it, and suspended above it was a rectangular frame draped in a mosquito net. The front of the net had been parted and pulled back over the corners, making it look invitingly like a canopy bed. In front of the bed was a round table with two chairs, and on the table was a pitcher of water with a lid, two upside down glasses, a lighter and a plate of candles.

I set my bags down. "Do I have this place to myself?" I asked.

"It's all yours, for now," replied Scott. "Depends on who else shows up."

We returned downstairs and left the house. I noticed that there was no lock, although there was a latch on the door. "Are we not going to lock the door?" I asked.

"I can give you a padlock if you want," replied Scott, "but we usually don't bother. People tend to respect each other's space and we haven't had any problems."

We hiked up the hill and returned to the platform where the native women sat with their wares. From there, a charming little bridge carried us across a gully to the main building. The main building was an enormous three story structure with a covered staircase on either side. It's design was open like the other buildings, but there was no netting on the outside walls. Unfortunately this meant that we would sometimes be bothered by insects. For that the air was fresh, the view unobstructed and we could urinate freely over the side.

I was taken aback the first time that Scott got up in mid sentence, walked to the edge, unzipped his pants and peed over the side. I asked him: "Is that a luxury reserved for the lord of the manor or is it a matter of doing in Rome as the Romans do?"

Scott laughed and said: "No, this is definitely Rome!"

From then on I peed outside every chance I got.

We climbed to the third floor of the main building, which was the only floor we ever used. The structure was built around a tree, growing up its center, so the floor was effectively divided into two rooms with connecting walkways at either end. One side was the dining room, and the other the chillout lounge. The chillout lounge was an open space with seven hammocks hanging from the rafters. We would spent most of our days there; reading, talking, snoozing and drinking coffee.

The dining area had a long table, set with tablecloths and earthenware china, that could accommodate ten people. Both the china and the cloths were decorated with artwork from the Shipibo Indians, who were a people known for their veneration of Ayahuasca. The artwork faithfully repeated curious line drawings–zig-zag patterns, arrows, hooks and strange shapes–that reminded me not of psychedelic visions but rather of circuit diagrams or symbolic codes. I imagined them being the product of an alien language glimpsed thousands of years ago which, not understood, was stylized and passed down through generations of shamans and artists.

Scott sat at the head of the table and I grabbed the seat next to him. He poured us coffee from a thermos and asked: "Do you mind if I smoke?"

"No, that's fine," I replied. He pulled a thick, filterless cigarette from his bag. "Do you role those yourself?" I asked.

"No," he said, "I buy these from someone. They're made with all natural tobacco and no additives. Do you smoke?"

"Only in lieu of pot," I said.

He reached into his bag and placed a handful of cigarettes on the table. "Try these," he said. "Do you need a lighter?" I nodded and he added a clear plastic lighter with a blue LED flashlight built into the bottom of it. "I get half a dozen of these for a dollar," he said.

An Indian woman came up the stairs with a bowl of soft white buns and a chicken vegetable omelet. Scott had already eaten, so it was all for me. The food was excellent and helped me settle in after my long trip. When I was finished I poured myself another coffee, pinched tobacco from the end of a cigarette and lit it. The tobacco was dark and course, and the smoke light and flavorful.

"This is the best cigarette I've ever had," I said. "Can you buy them like this in North America?"

"There's a brand called Natural American Spirit," he said, "which is similar." For a moment I saw myself becoming a smoker, but my enthusiasm wained after a couple of drags. I enjoyed the initial kick, but ultimately the feeling was empty. It felt unhealthy and failed to enhance my thoughts or perception in any way. I smoked half the cigarette and put the rest behind my ear for later.

A tall, broad shouldered man with a buzz cut came up the stairs and declared "Holy shit, I was up all night mun!" He pronounced "man" like "mun", so that it rhymed with sun. "I fought with demons all night, my house was full of 'em!" His name was Sam and he had an infectious, albeit nervous laugh. He had arrived the previous day and participated in his first Ayahuasca ceremony. He sat down and joined us for breakfast.

"It'll give you vivid dreams," agreed Scott. "Otto here is eager for his first ceremony. What do you think, are you ready for more?"

Sam laughed: "Fuck it, let's go mun; I don't need sleep!"

After breakfast we took our coffees to the chillout lounge and swayed in the hammocks until Jose, Scott's foreman, came by. Scott spoke with him in Spanish and then asked us "How would you like a tour of the property? I need to go to my office and process emails before my Internet connection cuts out in the afternoon."

We shrugged our shoulders and said "Sure, sounds good."

While Scott returned to his house, Sam and I followed Jose down the path. The weather was hot and the cigarettes that Scott had given me grew damp in the palm of my hand. When we came to my house I quickly jumped in, grabbed a sling bag and packed the cigarettes, a headlight, a windbreaker, mosquito repellent and a Swiss Army knife. I liked to be prepared.

Beyond my house the path was laid out with sticks and meandered like the tracks of an amusement ride through sun dappled jungle. I felt the soft, rich soil beneath the wood and thought of the millennia of biomass from countless plants and animals that had formed it. Along the path we paused on a bridge that arched across a pool of brown water, and watched the sun beam into it with honey golden shafts.

We came to a door at the base of a large tree. Jose unlocked it, and we followed him up an enclosed staircase that wound up the trunk to a house in the tree's branches, two stories above the forest floor. There was a large room with open windows, a leaf roof and platforms for beds. The structure felt remarkably sturdy, and Jose proudly told us that he had designed and constructed it himself. I asked where he had learned to build such a thing and he replied that the blueprints had been given to him in an Ayahuasca ceremony. The spirits had taught him how to build it.

"Aye mun, do you have a cigarette?" asked Sam.

I pulled one from my bag, handed it to him and lit the stub behind my ear for myself. The soft buzz returned. Jose leaned out the window, snapped a leaf from a leche caspi tree and showed us the milky white sap that welled forth. He caught a drip on his finger and licked it off.

"The sap is good against diarrhea," he explained. "Good for Ayahuasca."

I held out my finger and Jose put some on it. The sap was thick, creamy and sticky. I had some more, then sat back and took a drag from the cigarette. Jose, too, had lit one up, and our combined smoke wafted lazily out the window.

Jose lives like this, I thought. Here, in nature. No cars, no taxes, no laws, no dress code... it seemed wonderful. He lived from one project to the next and took his time doing it. When he needed guidance he took Ayahuasca, and who knew what other plants he communed with. He lived in harmony with himself and the environment. The structures he built were made from the plants themselves and not from hard, alien materials like concrete, glass or metal that rusted.

He showed us how the house was fastened to the tree not with nails, but with wire. The tree, he said, should not suffer from the construction. The culture that I came from would have cut the tree down, leveled the ground, paved over the soil and built a high-maintenance monstrosity. Maybe we'd add a strip of soil for degenerate ornamental flowers, but any medicinal or psychoactive plants would be outlawed. My heart sank at the thought of returning to Vancouver.

We left the tree house, walked up the hill and came to a generous slope of land with wide paths, clumps of trees and rectangular plots of neatly cultivated plants. This was "the garden"; a place where Scott grew whatever he needed. Jose pointed to a man in the distance. "I'm the architect," he said, "and he's the gardener."

The gardener came over and shook our hands. He had dark, deeply wrinkled skin, baggy jeans and a woody growth on the back of his hand that I made sure not to touch. He showed us around and told us the uses of various plants. Sam and I were excited to see a coca plant, but chewing the leaves had little effect. When we chewed the small yellow flowers of the "Button de oro" bush, however, it completely numbed our mouths for a couple of minutes.

The gardener also showed us his house, which was a room on stilts at the upper edge of the garden. His mattress was on the floor behind a mosquito net, and his clothes lay folded in piles on the ground or were draped over cables that criss-crossed the room. Along the wall near the entrance stood two plastic buckets with lids, and a dozen recycled bottles. They were filled with the same beige-brown liquid I had seen at Scott's house.

It was noni juice: the fermented roots and fruits of the noni tree mixed with honey. Apparently it was extremely healthy, but it smelled like vomit. The gardener removed the lid from a bucket, dipped a cup into the beige swill and offered it to Sam. Sam took a sip, made a face and declared: "Holy shit mun!" The gardener laughed. I tried it next-it tasted like liquid puke-and Jose finished the cup. We thanked the gardener and continued on our way.

Jose led us up a path to a house we hadn't seen yet; it was Scott's office. Beside the building was an elevated platform with a satellite dish. Jose called out: "Hola!"

"Hola mi amigo!" replied Scott from upstairs. "Did you enjoy the gardens? Come on up!"

The three of us went upstairs and found Scott topless in his jeans and rubber boots, sitting at an open window on a wooden high chair that leaned precariously to one side. In front of him, on the large windowsill, was a notebook computer, a ring of keys, a bunched up maroon polo shirt and two glasses of water.

"I have to stay on top of these emails," groaned Scott. "If I leave them for a day or two, they build up and become unmanageable." He wrapped up what he was doing and then came down from his perch. We pulled up four chairs and sat in a circle.

A wave of exhaustion swept over me. I lit a cigarette, took a single drag and put it out again. It made me dizzy. Scott told us a few things to prepare us for the upcoming ceremony—how it worked and how we should approach it—but I could scarcely focus on his words. I only registered two things. One: that Ayahuasca cleared the chacras, each in turn from the base to the crown, and two: that the dose was measured in fractions of cups. Sam had taken half a cup the night before and would increase his dose to three quarters. My dose would be determined during the ceremony.

After the conversation we all left Scott's office and hiked to the main building for dinner. Along the way, Scott stopped off at his place to give me a pair of rubber boots. Dinner consisted of a cucumber and tomato salad with lemon and olive oil dressing, and a main course of rice with chicken and vegetables. We washed it down with blood red juice and coffee. Dark clouds filled the sky and dimmed the light as we ate, and unleashed a torrent of rain over the jungle. Water beat the foliage and poured from the edge of the leaf roof, but it didn't last long. Before the meal was finished the shower ended as abruptly as it had started.

After dinner, the ground was wet and the air humid as I walked to my house. I was grateful for the boots. The sky had cleared and the light had returned, but I did not know what time it was. Maybe four in the afternoon? I vowed to never again travel without a time piece. The plan was to sleep until Scott's sentinels—his guards—came by at 8pm to escort us to the ceremonial hall somewhere in the jungle. I was very excited!

Back at the house I went upstairs, took off my clothes and climbed down to the bathroom with my toiletry bag in hand and a towel slung over my shoulder. I enjoyed walking around naked in the warm air. I flossed, brushed my teeth, shaved with soap and took a cold shower. I felt reborn. I returned upstairs, hung the towel over the back of a chair and climbed into bed. I placed my headlight beside the pillow, closed the mosquito net and fell asleep.

A dream come true

The clowns

I awoke at dusk and stared through the netting into the dieing light of the jungle. What time was it? Would the sentinel know to come and get me? I closed my eyes for what felt like a moment and opened them with a start. As if someone had flipped a switch, the night had become pitch black and the din of insects filled the air. I felt abandoned. I feared that I had overslept, that the ceremony had started without me or that it had long since finished. I strapped on the headlight, jumped out of bed and lit a candle on the table. I pulled on my clothes, worried that the Adidas logo on my shirt might offend the shaman and then checked the boots for insects before stuffing my feet and pants into them. I packed a camping pillow, candle lantern, water bottle, self-inflating mattress, Swiss army knife and bug repellent. I draped a fleece over my arm, blew out the candle and climbed down the stairs and into the jungle.

Sweat ran down my sides and my heart pounded as I marched up the hill. My breath appeared in particulate white puffs in the beam of my headlight. That morning I had awoken in Houston, Texas, and now I was bumbling through the Amazon jungle in the middle of the night. It was so dark that I couldn't discern the tree tops from the overcast sky. It felt as if I was underwater or on an alien planet, and the shadows were rife with unknown predators.

Sam's house loomed silently into view. I stepped as close to the porch as I dared and whispered: "Psssssst! Sam! Are you up?"

"Yeah mun, what is it?" came the reply from within the structure.

"Do you have the time? I'm worried that we missed the ceremony."

"I have no idea. Hang on." A flashlight turned on upstairs and beamed around the room. Sam got up, picked up a few things and came downstairs. "I couldn't sleep anyway," he said, "lets go wait in the hammock lounge."

I was relieved to have company. We hiked up the path, past the dark shape of Scott's house and up to the third floor of the main building. Sam reclined in a hammock and lit a cigarette. I pulled the candle lantern from my bag and hooked it to the rope that attached my hammock to a rafter. The lantern swung on it's chain and swayed the shadows back and forth across the room. Insects fluttered against the glass, crawled in through the top and drowned in the wax.

Sam put out his second cigarette and declared: "It's getting late. I'll go see what's keeping Scott."

"Okay," I said, "I'll hold down the fort."

Sam's footsteps disappeared into the night and I stared into the rafters, basking in where I was and what was about to happen. I was in the Amazon, and I would take Ayahuasca.

Sam returned and said: "C'mon, it's time to go."

I switched on the headlight, collected my things and blew out the candle. I could not telescope and pack-up the lantern while the wax was molten, so I carried it gingerly by the chain. Sam led the way down a steep flight of stairs through a hatch in the floor, then along a covered ramp down to a clearing behind the building. From there we followed a faint path of trodden grass across the clearing and into the trees.

I noticed sparkles on the ground, bright and piercing like tiny diamonds. Thinking that they were reflections of moisture I crouched down to get a better look, and discovered that they were the sharp glint of spiders' eyes. Thank God I was wearing boots! A few steps on, among the trees, I noticed soft orange reflections in the eyes of moths and small birds.

The path sloped gently up into another clearing and at its top, embedded in a wall of trees, stood the ceremonial hall. It was a wide structure with a plush conical roof that more than doubled its height. At its front was the mouth of a covered staircase that curved from the ground up to a mysterious glow on the second floor. We walked up the stairs and entered a round room, about twelve meters across. Three candles, waxed directly to the planks of the floor, flickered at its center.

A wall mounted bench ran around the room, interrupted only by the doorway to the staircase and to the bathroom. Pastel blue and green vomit basins were distributed beneath the seats. The wall reached only half way from the floor to the roof, creating an open gap all the way around the room. When you sat on the bench, the wall ended at your shoulder blades. The weight of the roof was carried by pillars which were integrated into- and extended beyond the wall every couple of meters.

"Good evening," said Scott from behind a small table at the far end. His bags were on the bench beside him, and beside those sat Ricardo, the shaman. Ricardo was a small dark man with a clean-shaven face and a conservative part in his shiny black hair. He wore an off-white robe adorned with a pattern of thin black lines and symbols.

"May I watch?" I asked, cautiously approaching the table.

Scott turned to the shaman and looked amused. "Sure," he said. He waxed three candles to the tabletop, lit them and began unpacking his bags. "This is Ayahuasca," he said. He held up a thick glass bottle with an opaque, orange brown liquid in it and set it on the table. Next to it he placed slim bottles of "Agua de Florida"; floral water. He added a stemmed plastic goblet, a mug, a thermos with coffee, a bottle of water, a pile of cigarettes and a couple of lighters.

"How do we proceed?" I asked.

"Come with me," he said. He got up and led the way to the bathroom with his flashlight. We crossed a small bridge and entered an adjoining room with a concrete floor. Mounted to the floor were three white toilets, generously spaced side by side. The one on the far left looked in tact, the next one had no lid on the tank and the third had neither tank nor toilet seat. None of them had running water and there was no door in the frame.

"Let me know if you need to go to the bathroom during the ceremony, and I'll take you here," he said. We returned to the main room.

"Where should I sit?" I asked.

"We sit up against the poles," said Scott. "I'd recommend a seat close to the bathroom. You can purge in the toilet, into the basin or over the back of the bench into the forest. Being on the second floor had its advantages: there are less insects, the air is fresher and the vomit falls out of sight."

Scott returned to his seat and put on a robe similar to the shaman's. I took off my boots, inflated the mattress and unstuffed the camping pillow. I laid my fleece, water, repellent and vomit basin to my right, placed the mattress on the bench and the pillow to my back, and sat cross-legged against the pole. I tightened the bungee straps on the cuffs of my pants and sprayed repellent on my socks, arms and neck.

"We recommend a smaller dose for the first time," Scott called across the floor.

"I feel strong and brave," I replied, "and I'm fairly experienced with altered states of consciousness."

"Then let's start you off on a three quarter cup," reasoned Scott. "That's quite a lot. If you don't feel anything after an hour we can increase the dosage."

Scott poured himself half a goblet of Ayauasca, breathed on it in deep concentration, said "Salut!" and drank it. He then poured one for Ricardo, who did the same.

"Sam," said Scott in a low voice.

Sam, who had been sitting in quiet meditation on the other side of the room, walked up and knelt respectfully beside the table. They whispered in the candlelight and Sam drank a cup. He then returned to his seat, took a deep breath, belched and spat into the bucket.

"Otto."

I walked up slowly and Scott indicated I should sit beside him on the bench. Shadows danced on the table. Carefully he poured the medicine to the level that he felt was right for me. The goblet reminded me of a container one might use to hold paint in an art class. The inside was orange and the outside was brown, and a drip of orange had run down the side during manufacture.

Scott closed his eyes and breathed on the surface of the liquid. Then he extended it to me and whispered "Drink this."

I took the goblet, placed it to my lips and swallowed it in one go. The Ayahuasca was thick and terribly bitter. It tasted like heartburn and tobacco. Scott took the goblet from my hands and gave me a cup of steaming black coffee. "This'll help keep it down," he whispered. The hot liquid soothed my throat. He patted my shoulder and indicated I should take my seat.

I walked back and sat cross-legged against the pole. My gut gurgled. I wanted to spit into the basin as Sam had done, but dared not for fear of triggering regurgitation. I breathed deeply and tried to relax.

Scott went over to Sam, did something with him and then came over to me. He poured Agua Florida on his hands, drew crosses on my forehead, throat and the back of my neck, smeared it on the sides of my face and dabbed a line under my nose. The smell reminded me of 4711 Eau de Cologne. He turned my palms face up, sprinkled Agua Florida on them with his thumb over the mouth of the bottle, and blew on them. My palms grew cold. He placed my hands together as if in prayer, repeated the procedure on the outside and then told me to cup my hands over my nose and breath the pungent vapor.

Scott returned to his seat and sat in silence. The ceremony was a patient affair. After a while he mumbled a prayer in Spanish, got up, walked to the candles in the middle of the room and extinguished them with rustling shakes from a fan made of dry leaves. He then went back and did the same to the candles on the table.

There we were: in a dark room in the middle of the Amazon, in the middle of the night. I listened to the insects and stared at the faint strip of moonlit jungle glowing across my field of vision. I heard a noise, and saw Scott's silhouette move around the room with the glowing cherry of a cigarette. It grew brighter when he took a drag and I smelled a warm puff of tobacco as he walked by.

Ricardo sighed in high pitched tones, presumably feeling the effects of the drug and warming up his vocal chords. Vague blotches of color appeared in the darkness. I encouraged them to intensify and take form, but they remained little more than the static one ordinarily sees when the lights are out. This did not change when Ricardo broke into his primal, haunting song.

Footsteps approached and I felt Scott stand in front of me. He took a swig from a bottle, took my head in his hands and blew a spray of Agua Florida where my crown chakra would be. Cool liquid ran down my scalp. He did this repeatedly throughout the ceremony, and also blew it along my torso and down my arms.

After an hour, Sam stirred in his corner and his silhouette came into view. I heard a retching sound, a splattering on leaves and his voice gasping "Oh God!" This went on for a while.

After two hours, Scott came up and whispered "How are you feeling?"

"I feel fine," I replied, trying not to sound disappointed. "I don't feel anything."

"Would you like some more?"

"Sure," I said. He took me by the arm and I protested: "I can walk fine."

Scott chuckled: "Then walk."

I sat down beside him again and he filled the cup half way using the blue light in the bottom of his lighter. I drank it and washed it down with coffee. "Okay," he said, and I returned to my seat.

Nothing happened. The bilious liquid churned in my gut and with it grew my contempt for Ayahuasca and shamanism. "I've had more profound experiences on a Friday night in my apartment!" I thought. I felt that I had plumbed the depths of the psychedelic experience and that this primitive ritual and impotent drug could teach me nothing.

Across the room, Sam breathed heavily, belched and hummed in a wispy high pitch. I considered going over and checking on him, but then thought better of it. I did not want to offend ceremonial protocol.

Scott got up, crossed the room and walked down the stairs into the jungle. "Where's he going?" I thought. "Is the ceremony over?" Quietly I crept across the floor to where I could watch him, glowing milky white in his robe. The sky had cleared and the moon beamed like a floodlight. Scott walked around, looked up at the sky, peed in the open and came back in. I returned to my seat, placed the mattress on the floor and lay down for a snooze.

Rifle shots cracked in the jungle. It was Scott's sentinels signaling that it was midnight, that the ceremony was over and that the grounds were secure, but I didn't know that yet. I stretched and sat up. Scott said a prayer to dispel the spirits, walked to the middle of the room and lit the candles. Then he came over and sat on the bench next to me.

"How did it go?" he asked.

"I saw some vague blotches of color," I said, "but otherwise nothing happened."

"Then you'll have to try more next time," he replied, "although you took quite a bit tonight. You had more than our friend across the room. Ayahuasca is a feminine spirit and can be coy; she may not show herself right away. We shouldn't discount her yet, though; you still have the night ahead of you."

This did not sit well with me at all. I expected a drug to work in an orderly, masculine fashion. I did not care for capriciousness in my psychedelic experience.

"How's Sam doing?" I asked. "I was tempted to go over and check on him during the ceremony, but then I figured that might breach the protocol."

"It's good that you didn't," he said, "participants need their space. Sam had a rough night. We'll give him some time to collect himself."

Scott went off to pack his things and I set about deflating the mattress. When we were ready we picked up Sam, blew out the candles and left the hall. Ricardo had long since hurried off to join a Christmas party at a nearby village.

The night was incredible. The moon gleamed like a silver coin and the stars washed across the sky like sparkling milk. I left my headlight off.

"How did your night go?" I asked Sam.

"Holy shit mun," he breathed, "I died twice. I thought I took too much and lost my mind."

"Was Scott not able to help you, or the shaman's song?"

"Scott couldn't do shit for me," he said bitterly. "I was beyond anyone's reach. I was trapped in hell, in a dungeon, and spiders and demons were gnawing at me. At one point, cracks appeared all around me and light beamed in, and I thought an angel was coming to save me. But then a giant bloodshot eye peered in from the other side, and claws reached through and tried to open the gap." He shuddered and huddled his arms around himself. "My skin feels like it's stuck to my bones."

"You lost a lot of water tonight," remarked Scott.

When we came to the main building I discovered that the path went not around, but straight through it. Within the structure we found a pitcher of lemonade and glasses that had been set out for us on a table. It was a thoughtful touch and wonderfully refreshing after four hours of bitter Ayahuasca. Sam was especially grateful for the hydration. We took a breather, drained our glasses and marched on.

Next to the platform where the women had sat throughout the day, we encountered a man in a yellow jacket with a rifle slung over his shoulder. Scott went over and talked to him in Spanish. When he was finished he reached into his bag and gave the man a handful of cigarettes.

Scott explained: "My sentinels guard the territory throughout the night."

"Do they guard against humans or animals?" I asked.

"People," replied Scott. "If someone enters my property without my permission, I shoot at them."

We stopped off at Scott's place to get a blanket for Sam who was shivering with cold, and then continued down the path to Sam's house. Sam smiled weakly when we arrived at his porch and wished us a good night. He gave me an awkward hug with his head braced against my chest. "Sorry about my wet clothes," he said.

"No worries," I told him. "Sleep tight, everything will be better in the morning." I patted him on the shoulder and was amazed how damp it was. We watched Sam enter the house and then Scott and I continued down the hill.

"And then there were two," I said. The jungle grew denser and darker as we walked, and the pulse of zany electronic music rose in the distance. "What's going on there?" I asked.

"That's the Christmas party," said Scott.

"Can we check it out?" I asked, eager for some action.

"It'll have degenerated to a drunken brawl at this point," he said. "The locals are impoverished and their lives cycle from toil to intoxication. They are at a construction worker level of existence."

Scott led the way into my house and up the stairs, and lit a candle on the table in front of the bed. I paused and shined my light on a large spider on the floor. "What about this guy?" I asked.

Scott came over and examined it. "These fall from the roof sometimes, but this one looks dead. Actually, this might be a shell. Spiders shed their skins much like snakes do, but they leave behind a full body skeleton that looks like the real thing."

I had never heard of that. Scott nudged it with his foot and it appeared to move. "Maybe not, maybe it's real. Well then," he said, and stepped on it with a crunch.

We sat down at the table. "How is it possible," I asked, "for Ayahuasca to have no effect on me, even after a second dose? No matter how distracted you are, you can't hide from a large dose of LSD, mushrooms or alcohol. They will get you undeniably high whether you want it or not."

"It's usually the same with Ayahuasca," conceded Scott, "but you have to understand that Ayahuasca is more than just a chemical: it has a spiritual component. That's why it's so important to have a structured ceremony and to send away the spirits at the end. You're not fully here yet. The memories of your trip and the novelty of the ceremony give you an identity beyond the here and now. You're busy processing and not open to the experience. However, once I leave and your mind quiets down, the medicine may still manifest. You may be in for an interesting evening!"

"Yeah, the Ayahuasca is still heavy in my gut," I agreed. "I may have to throw up before the night is through."

He gave me a hug. "I'm glad you're finally here," he said. "One of the girls will bring you fruit and tea in the morning." He climbed down the stairs and banged the door shut on his way out.

I stood for a while and collected my thoughts. I was in a mesh house in the Amazon, with boots on my feet, a light on my head and a candle on the table. I could smell the rough blond wood of which the floor and frame were made. It was well past midnight, probably past one, which meant I had taken Ayahuasca over four hours ago. I was utterly exhausted and remarkably sober.

I removed the boots, pulled off the steamy socks and scrutinized the floor as I climbed barefoot down the stairs to the bathroom. After assuring myself that the rim and the water of the toilet were free of snakes, spiders and insects, I pulled down my pants, sat down and gratefully released the pressure that had built up in my gut. I stared at my pink feet on the cool concrete, and noticed a black beetle on the floor between the wall and the toilet. It lay on its back and a dozen ants bustled around it. "A lovely image of death and decay," I thought.

I turned off the headlight to conserve the battery. The room went dark and the jungle glowed blue through the gaps in the wall. I rested my elbows on my knees, hung my head and closed my eyes, and listened to the trills, ticks, clicks, pops and buzzes of the insects. They made noises like electric hair clippers, like computers starting up and like motors turning over. Their sounds were mechanical and alien, and their meaning was as obscure to me as the thoughts and feelings in their compound eyes and armored faces. I imagined how lit up the jungle would be if every insect clinging to every leaf were to glow in the night like a firefly.

I took a deep breath and relaxed my muscles, and then something began to happen. The sounds grew louder and skipped and echoed. My heart pounded, my skin grew numb and luminous threads rained down from the ceiling. I felt like I would pass out and barely managed to wipe and pull up my pants before stumbling forward and collapsing on the strip of wooden floor in front of the mirror. The zany dance music from the nearby village played hideously backwards in my ears like a maniacal fun house. My eyes were blinded as by a strobe light flashing white, yellow and red into my face. I launched into a vast white void teeming with frenetic clowns, candy ambulances with over-sized lights and bells, and brightly colored objects that flashed in and out of existence. They darted around so quickly that I could barely see them.

I don't know how to convey the aggressive assault of this experience. Never before had I been so overwhelmed! In under a minute I went from dozing off on the toilet in the middle of the night to having my senses overloaded in an electric crystalline asylum. There was no pulling back from it; no sanctuary from the insane frenzy. Cupping my ears and clenching my eyes had no effect. I gasped for breath and yawned uncontrollably. Deranged hyper-dimensional clowns flooded my nervous system and toyed with the structures of my mind.

"Holy shit, what have I done?!" I thought. "This is not what I wanted!"

I was alone like never before, tripping-out on a bathroom floor in the Peruvian Amazon. I had abandoned my girlfriend, friends and family for this, and on Christmas no less. I had turned away from all who cared for me and willfully embarked on this journey to the edge of consciousness. Me-me-me. I had kissed a girl in Houston and proudly posted it on my blog for Natalia to read; Natalia who had failed a medical exam and started taking anti-depressants the day I left. I imagined her alone in cold gray Vancouver, driven to suicide at that very moment by pain and betrayal.

I wanted to hike to Scott's house and ask to use his Internet connection to tell Natalia how much she meant to me, but it was impossible. It was the middle of the night and I was completely incapacitated. I lay on the floor for over an hour, and every second was a screaming eternity. I wished that Scott or the shaman could have been there for me.

"What have I done to my life?!" I thought. "What have I done to my brain?! First thing tomorrow, if I make it through this, I'm going to leave the Refugio and book the next flight home!"

I had to come to my senses! I crawled to the toilet, sobbed into the bowl and strained to throw up, but nothing came. The Ayahuasca had long since absorbed into my system. Like Sam had said about his experience: nothing could help me. I had to ride it out. Church bells rang in an endless demented loop and neon patterns washed across the inky floor.

I became angry. "Fuck you, you fucking clowns!" I whispered in the dark. "Get out of my head!!!" I groped around for my light but found nothing. "Fuck it," I said, "I'm going to bed."

I climbed the stairs on all fours, threw my clothes on a chair and slipped into bed. The bells still rang, the lights still flashed and the clowns still raged, but it had become more manageable. My heart ached with regret for the love I had withheld and the ungrateful person I had been, and that's when I realized what the clowns had given me to understand. I curled into a ball and thanked them for all they had taught me.

Despite my fatigue, I was not able to fall asleep. My mind buzzed and buzzed, and I thought: "I must record these memories before they fade!" Grudgingly I got out of bed, climbed down to the bathroom and retrieved the headlight. I then rummaged through my bags for the diary, but couldn't find it.

"I guess it's not meant to be," I thought. "I'm too tired to write anyway, let alone formulate a sentence. What was I thinking?!"

I lay back down and closed my eyes, but sleep refused to come. Dawn crept into the jungle as I played the evening over and over in my thoughts. "Alright, dammit!" I said, pulled myself up for another search and found the zip-lock bag with my diary and fountain pen. With eyes half closed and my mind swimming in details, I made a list of all that had happened: from when Natalia drove Andrei and me to the airport to where I was now, sitting cross legged in bed. It felt like one very, very long day. When I was done I returned the book and pen to the bag, and placed it together with the headlight beside the pillow. Finally my mind released its grip on the day's events, and I drifted into slumber.

Christmas day

After a few hours of shallow sleep I opened my eyes and saw through the mosquito net that someone had set a jug of fennel tea and a plate of sliced bananas, papayas and apples on the table next to the bed. The sun was out and the insects and clowns had quieted down. I got up, poured myself some tea and removed the saran wrap from the plate. The fruits were soft and smelly. I picked out the apples and scraped the rest over the porch into the bushes below.

I took a brisk shower, washed the Agua Florida from my hair, got dressed and hiked up the hill to the main building. As I emerged from the stairs on to the third floor, I saw Sam sitting alone at the table and smoking a cigarette.

"Holy shit!" I declared without saying good morning, and launched excitedly into my ordeal with the clowns. Sam listened for about a minute and then broke in: "Woe mun, you look traumatized!"

"You're right," I said, and paused to take a breath. I realized that I was assaulting him with my story. "I'm sorry," I continued more slowly, "it scared the crap out of me. I was on the verge of walking out of the Refugio today." I poured myself coffee and waited for the staff to bring me breakfast. The weather was warm and pleasant.

Scott came up the stairs and joined us at the table. "Good morning!" he announced cheerfully.

"Hi Scott, I had a rough night after you left," I said, and recounted the night's events in broad strokes.

Scott nodded. "It's not uncommon to feel an intense need to speak with loved ones after your first ceremony," he said. "A factor in this is that we worry about other people to keep from focusing on ourselves."

"Would it be possible for me to use the Internet today?" I asked.

"We'll go down to the office in the afternoon," he assured me.

We finished our breakfast and then continued the conversation in the chillout lounge.

"One time, after a ceremony," said Scott, "a guy in the next house called to me in the middle of the night: 'Hey Scott! There's a cat in my room!'

"I told him 'Shine a light on it!' and he called back: 'I tried, but it runs away and hides!'

"'Then it's nothing, it won't hurt you!' I said. 'Go to sleep!'

"You see, the visions are just holograms. Stay detached and watch them like you watch a movie, and never lose your sense of humor! Smile at whatever happens, because nothing disempowers a demon more than laughing at it. If something ghastly appears, say 'my, don't you look grim today,' and move on. Anything you give attention to will gain in strength."

"Does anyone ever get hurt?" I asked. "Do people ever jump from windows to escape their visions?"

"Sometimes," he said. "A guy once freaked out because he couldn't find his wallet. He jumped up, ran into a wall, fell over the railing and broke his arm. The shaman then turned to me and said: 'Leave him be, let him look for his wallet down there!' The ground was a better place for him and he was fine for the rest of the ceremony.

"Ayahuasca is an evolutionary aid and has your best interests at heart, but it doesn't respect teetotalers. You have to jump in with both feet. Some people believe they're being manipulated by demons and say 'Fuck this, I'm going back to church!', and they'll hide from something all their lives. You can't know heaven without knowing hell. You'll be half a person, and if that's what you want to protect your fears, go for it. A lot of people do. They'll think 'The reason I'm all fucked-up is because of him,' when in fact the only thing that controls us is ourselves. When you realize this, it is incredibly liberating. No longer are you a leaf in the wind. You can achieve anything if you keep at it and sacrifice everything that gets in your way. The spirit always leads, and thoughts become things."

We finished our coffees, left the main building and walked through muggy, oxygen rich jungle to the office. Scott retrieved his laptop from a cupboard, set it up on the windowsill and pressed the power button. "Go ahead," he said.

I mounted the rickety highchair and pulled out my diary and memory stick while the boot animation scrolled by. A quivering line of pixels bisected the damaged screen. "So, this runs on solar power and satellite access?" I remarked, impressed with the self-sufficiency.

"Yes," he said, "the sun provides plenty of power. We'll soon get the lights working in the houses too. The satellite's a different story, though. I've had the guys out a couple of times but it still cuts out in the afternoon."

Scott pointed to a jug on a table. "There's water here if you need it," he said. "I'm going to take care of things for about an hour. Will that be enough time for you?"

"That'll be great, thank you," I said.

Scott went downstairs and out the door.

I stared into the sunny foliage beyond the computer and reflected on what Scott had achieved. He had beaten his own path through the jungle of life and founded not only a place of healing, but his own kingdom. Regardless whether I wanted to live the way he did, alone in a foreign country in an underdeveloped society, he was among the rare humans who blossom to their full potential.

As I sat and mused, a spindly black creature with luminescent blue appendages floated in through the window. It was scarcely larger than my thumb nail and looked more like an alien spacecraft than an insect. A familiar morphology—with wings, legs and antennae sprouting from a three-part body—was not apparent. It consisted of two central columns, like a catamaran, within a symmetrical framework of fuzzy black insectoid girders. I thought it might be two insects clinging to each other, but it moved as one and never separated.

The thing hovered around as if examining me. I aimed my camera at it but it dodged the line of sight, so I took wild snapshots in its direction. Each flash knocked the creature back in the air, and the camera caught little more than dark blurs and luminescent smudges. Finally, when the insect came too close, I batted it with my hand and it floated back out the window.

I returned my attention to the laptop. I emailed Natalia that I was sorry and told her, for the first time, that I loved her. That was a big step for me and I knew that she needed to hear it. Then I emailed my buddy Steve and asked him to look in on Natalia. I would have liked to tell him that I loved him too, and my mother for that matter, but that would have gone too far. In some relationships, some feelings are better left understood than spelled out.

When I was finished I leaned back and breathed a sigh of relief. I marveled at how my will had, through mouse clicks and keystrokes, manipulated electrons and created emissaries that would reach to Vancouver, communicate my feelings and right my wrongs.

I don't recall how the day went by after that, but it ended with Sam, Scott and I smoking pot and raising glasses of sweet champagne to Christmas day on Scott's balcony. Scott swayed in his hammock, Sam and I lounged in wooden armchairs, and between us stood a table with candles, glasses and bottles.

"What brought you to the Amazon?" I asked Scott.

"When you decide on a spiritual path, a path of exploration," he replied, "it never leaves you. You may think you've arrived, but it keeps coming. I had been in the healing business for many years, and recognized a need for my art as our planet and culture deteriorated. I was also familiar with getting things done in the third world."

"How is getting things done in the third world different from getting them done elsewhere?"

"I'm like a plantation owner," he explained, "and that requires a master-servant mentality. You have to be dominant, certain and strong. The workers must be told clearly and directly what to do, otherwise they won't do it. They want to be led, and they are kept in line with money, respect, force and fear. They fear me because they think I'm a witch. They think we're all witches, doing what we're doing."

His very bluntness revealed the uncompromising plantation owner mentality that Scott was talking about. It sounded harsh and politically incorrect, but I think the locals regarded him as a benevolent father. Scott provided jobs and income to over twenty families. He circulated books, supported projects, financed parties and handed out Christmas baskets with chocolate, champagne and panettone.

"What exactly are we doing?" I asked. "From a western perspective, we're taking drugs to alter our thoughts and perceptions. That alone might suffice to explain a profound experience, but with Ayahuasca there's all this talk of spirits and the spirit world. Can you explain this to me?"

"People think that if you can't nail it and can't weld it, it doesn't exist," replied Scott. "Neural theory has validity and brain chemistry is a useful paradigm, but there's more to human beings than meets the scientific eye. Western medicine is defensive and has a frightened insistence on physicality. How many pills will it take to keep citizens walking straight in a world of rising depression, aggression and suicide? There's a lot of information that science cannot deal with. Shamanism wants to improve the system, not invalidate science."

"Then, where and what are spirits? Do they live all around us in the physical world, like air? Does Ayahuasca make them visible to us like a flashlight illuminates furniture in a dark room?"

"No." said Scott firmly. "San Pedro, Peyote and Psilocybin Mushrooms transform the world into a magical wonderland, but Ayahuasca shows you something internal. Waking reality is like a campfire that humanity huddles around, and Ayahuasca extinguishes that fire. It allows you to perceive the forest which the flames prevented you from seeing.

"Think of it in terms of perception rather than vision. You may smell a snake, hear it and know it's there without seeing it. A common theme is the feeling that something is coming up behind you, but don't worry about it unless you feel a hand on your shoulder. We react in atrophied capacities—like animal perception when we hunt—and filter the spiritual dimension through our personal psychology, beliefs and experiences."

"Do we meet the souls of the dead as the name Ayahuasca implies?"

"Some spirits may be from the deceased, but the spirit realm existed long before humans did. It is a complex network of energies, some friendly and some hostile just as there are different people. If a spirit tells you that it is your long lost relative, don't believe it. The spirits are tricksters, and they will toy with you the way a brat toys with a retarded child."

Scott paused for a toke and a sip of champagne before continuing. "I appreciate what you're doing," he said. "Your pedantic questions document what this is all about and prepare you for the ceremony, but you're barking up the wrong tree. Buying into someone else's view, theory or religion is not the right way. You need to connect to your own spirit and discover your own idea of God, otherwise you won't believe it. You won't have confidence and it won't empower you.

"Don't worry, you just arrived. We'll have another go at it tomorrow."

Power animals

The next morning I felt remarkably hungover as I joined Sam, Scott and a middle aged British couple at the breakfast table.

"I can't believe how out of it I feel," I groaned, "I didn't drink or smoke that much."

"Ayahuasca can get jealous," explained Scott. "It'll make you feel like you have a cold and turn your learning into a gray cloud. You should wait three days before consuming other drugs."

I remembered reading on the Internet that Ayahuasca abruptly cured drug addictions.

I stared into space and sipped my coffee, and listened to the British couple talk about fairies. After a while I turned to them and said "I'm sorry, I couldn't help but overhear your conversation about fairies, and it struck me that you speak of them as if they actually exist. Is that right?"

"Certainly they exist!" replied the man. "What did you think?"

"Well," I said thoughtfully, "that depends on how we define existence. Anything I think has a life in my thoughts and can likely be measured in my brain activity, but that is existence of the idea and not the thing itself. I never considered fairies to have substance beyond that."

"They do exist," he assured me. "Have you not seen them in the ceremony?"

"No," I said, "but I've only had one ceremony and that didn't go as planned. When I got back to my house I was attacked by clowns, and I can't even vouch that those were real."

"My God, man! Do you not believe your own eyes?"

"I suppose I don't, at least not on a single viewing. Our senses can play tricks on us and extraordinary claims require extraordinary proof. I think it's reckless to believe things on a whim and without solid evidence."

"Then," declared the man with satisfaction, "you cannot believe in love."

"Why not?" I replied. "There's good reason to believe in love. It's a familiar feeling for most people, I have been in love myself and even science recognizes it."

The man's face turned grim. "Why are you here?" he asked. "Do you want to piss on everyone's parade?"

His wife gently cut in: "Let's see what tonight's ceremony brings."

"Yes," I agreed. "Please don't get me wrong: I would love for fairies to exist. I just haven't seen them yet."

I took my coffee and joined Sam in the hammock lounge. He offered me a cigarette and I declined; I'd lost the taste for it. I pulled out my diary and tried to express the conflict that I felt. This was the second time that my reasoning had been criticized, and that brought to the surface that I too was troubled by the bloodless sterility of my thoughts. There was nothing I wanted more than to see the world brimming with fairies, gnomes, spirits and aliens, but my paradigm did not allow it. It felt as if a colorful beast was trapped in my chest, caged behind the bars of my meticulously maintained model of the world.

Sam jumped out of his hammock and shouted "Fuck mun, a spider bit me!" I rushed over and helped him pat down his clothes and search the floor, but we found nothing.

"Where did it get you?" I asked.

"It didn't hurt at first," he said, sitting down in another hammock and pulling up his left foot. "I thought it was a mosquito, but then– shit, look at that!" He showed me two bloody puncture marks on the tip of his big toe. "What if it was poisonous?!"

"Let's go see Scott," I said, "I think he's at his office. Don't worry, it's probably nothing."

Sam put on his sandals and together we marched down the hill. His pace betrayed how worried he was; I could barely keep up. When we came to the office we found a padlock in the latch, and our calls were met with silence.

"Shit mun," breathed Sam, "I think my toe is going numb!" He was pale and winded.

"Don't worry," I said, "my legs feel numb too after speedwalking down here. Scott's probably at his house. Let's walk back, but let's slow down a bit. If there is poison in your system it's probably a good idea to keep your heart rate down."

"Okay mun!" he nodded, and rushed up the hill. When Scott's house came into view I shouted "Scott! Sam got bitten by something on his foot!"

"Come on up, let's have a look at it," came the reply from his hammock. We went upstairs and sat in the same chairs as the night before. Scott cleaned Sam's toe with a disinfecting wipe, examined the foot and the ankle, and declared the bite harmless.

"If it was toxic," he said, "it would move into the ankle, up the back of the leg, swell the lymph nodes in the groin and armpit, cross over the head and move down the other side."

"Why does Sam look so pale?" I asked.

"It's the excitement," he said. "It's important to remain calm and detached at all time, both in the ceremony and in real life. Sam also has issues with his lungs, for which we're making medicine today. We were about to get started."

"Can I watch?" I asked.

"Sure," he said. "Sam, why don't you rest here for a bit."

"Okay, thanks," agreed Sam. He sighed and sat back in the chair.

I followed behind Scott. He picked up a bowl and a machete, went outside and walked over to Jose who was scrutinizing the trees along the path.

"What are we looking for?" I asked.

"Termites," said Scott.

"You're going to make medicine out of insects?"

"Everything is energy," he said, "no matter what form it takes. Termites are excellent for bronchial problems. Not just termites, but their larva and nest material."

He pointed out a brown mass, over a meter across, bulging from the side of a nearby tree. Vein-like structures radiated from the nest and ran along the trunk down to the ground. Jose fetched a ladder and held it against the tree, and Scott climbed up and chipped away the surface with his machete.

"We want the fresh material," he called down, "not the dry stuff!"

With the tip of the blade, he carved moist dark chunks from the center of the nest and caught them in the bowl. When the vessel was full he climbed down, carried it to the main building and set it down on the wooden floor. The bowl teemed with excited little termites. Scott picked up a wooden pestle and pounded the material.

"You have to mash it until all the termites are dead and everything is a powder," he said.

He poured hot water into the bowl, let it steep for a moment and then strained the mixture through a cloth into a second bowl. The resulting liquid was beige and the steam had a sweet smell. Scott took three clear glass bottles, filled them half way with liquid honey, added a quarter of termite brew and topped it off with lemon juice. He shook one up and handed it to me.

"Here you go," he said. "When you write about this, please mention that I have plenty more tricks than this!"

I took a swig and it tingled in the back of my throat. It tasted like honey, lemon and sweet wood. Sam emerged from Scott's house and came over.

"How's your toe?" I asked.

"It's fine," replied Sam, "but I think it was a sign. I think the spiders from my last session are communicating with me. Last night I had a spiderweb beside my bed, this morning I found a dead spider on the floor and now a spider bit me on the left side of my body, which is the feminine and spiritual side."

I thought about the spider I had found on the floor after the first ceremony, and about how slippery a thing it was to project meaning into things.

"Spiders are spinners of webs," said Scott.

"What do you mean by that?" I asked.

"Every animal has a gift," he explained, "and often times the strongest traits are in the smallest animals. Spiders spin webs of silk but they also spin webs of thought. They are weavers of stories and relationships. They are also symbols of malignancy."

"How can an animal give a gift?"

"By choosing you and sharing with you it's greatest power. It's a reciprocal relationship. It bonds you to nature and bridges your conscious and subconscious minds."

"Can any animal be a spirit animal?"

"The traditional power animals of the Amazon are the black snake, black panther, stingray and electric eel, but every animal has its virtue. Tribal cultures benefit from traits such as speed and aggression, but modern shamans tend toward animals with more subtle qualities. Since everything has spirit, you can conceivably bond with anything; not just an animal. You could bond with the moon or a stone. For that matter, you could even bond with another human."

Second ceremony

"I'm sitting in restless anticipation of what tonight's ceremony will bring. The night is black and the air is thick with the hypnotic buzz of insects. It reaches high into the trees and deep into the jungle, and is bound by the incessant chirring of cicadas as the ocean binds all that live within it. Periodically, something unseen passes overhead and flaps like a flag in the wind. A

phenomenal abundance of plant and animal life
and we humans are just another creature among
them, emerged from the ground to return to it."

Those were my impressions as I sat at the dining table and
wrote by the light of my candle lantern. As before the first
ceremony, I had awoken early and marched up the hill
to the main building. This time, however, I was neither
worried that I had overslept nor did I disturb Sam as I
went by his house. It was my third day and third night
at the Refugio, and I had found comfort in its rhythm.
I closed the diary, shut my eyes and let the sounds carry
me away.

After a while I was roused by voices and saw the beams
of flashlights moving up the path to the ceremonial hall.
I packed up and followed them. As I entered the hall,
candles glowed at it's center and Scott, Ricardo, Sam and
the British couple settled into their seats. I went over to
my pole and prepared for the ceremony.

Scott started me off on more medicine than in the
first ceremony—seven eighths of a cup instead of three
quarters—but never offered seconds so that I ended up
drinking less in total. Aside from that, things progressed
much as they had before. The other participants vomited
within two hours, and I sat in the dark with a gurgling
gut and felt nothing.

I yawned, stretched my hands up behind the pole and
felt a curious vein on the wood. I pressed on it and it
collapsed with a satisfying crunch. I moved my fingers

along and kept pushing it in until a sweet smell, familiar from the termite juice, reached my nose. Realizing that I was destroying an insect tunnel, I stopped and put my hands in my lap. After a moment, little things started crawling up my neck, down my shirt and along my hairline. I brushed them off, shook out my hair and moved over to the next pole.

The rifles fired at midnight, the prayer was said and we packed up and left the hall. I felt queasy and carried a basin with me back to my house so that I might throw up in the comfort of my bed. Scott walked with me, but we didn't connect the way we had the first night. We were both in our heads. I was frustrated that the stuff wasn't working and Scott was unfocused and rambled on mostly about himself. He said that my immunity might be tied to my mind; to my analytic perspective. "The visuals do not like to be scrutinized," he said.

I worried that the clowns would again jump me once Scott left, but nothing happened. I went to bed with the basin beside my feet and slept the night through.

Blue and yellow threads

When I awoke in the morning I stared into the mosquito net and thought about how different people were. It was easy to lump us together as a race, a gender, a culture or a genome, but how much were we actually alike? How much were our thoughts and our sense of "I" the same? We shared impressions of the world, sensations of our bodies and memes of society, but all that was part of a shell. None of that was me. I was something apart from that, reaching out from deep beneath those layers.

As I looked within, I remembered how a thought had been compared in it's intangibility to a photon of light. It had no mass and no location, and it vanished as suddenly as it appeared. My focus shrank to something so small and so distant, that neighboring molecules twinkled like stars in the night sky. At that level, my mind was its own universe and my body extended light years beyond that. How similar or how near, then, was one person to another?

At breakfast, Sam shared with us that he had grown up in a bomb shelter in the middle east and watched glowing red bullets fly through the night. One time, he saw four people get pinned to the ground and shot in the head. The killers warned onlookers not to move the bodies for four days lest they too be shot.

"That's why your demons are especially large," said Scott, and then imitated Sam's anguished whimper from previous ceremonies. My eyes flashed to see how Sam would react, but he laughed it off. "There are gargoyles at the gate," continued Scott, "to keep out those who are not intended inside. That's probably for their own good."

"Hey Scott!" a voice called up from the path. Three young Swedes came up the stairs and introduced themselves as Johan, Camilla and Mikael. Mikael had been to the Refugio before. Scott got up and showed them to their house, and they returned when the rest of us had finished breakfast and eased into hammocks with our coffees.

Mikael carried a book with him–Antipodes of the Mind, by Benny Shanon–which he praised as the Ayahuasca bible. I opened the book and was intrigued by an allegory which the author had apparently been told by a Peruvian ice cream vendor. It said that God wanted a place to hide his secrets. He considered hiding them on the moon or in the oceans, but feared that one day a non-deserving human might find them there. Eventually he found the perfect hiding place, and buried his secrets in the depths of man's own mind. That way, only those who were worthy could reach them.

Is that what we were doing: accessing God's secrets in our minds? Perhaps the secret was, beneath all the layers, that we were God. We spoke of such and other things until the next meal, and after that we retired to our beds in preparation for the next ceremony.

After a few hours of deep sleep, I awoke to the sound of rain pouring on the roof and the foliage of the jungle. The sheets were damp, and I pictured the moisture seeping like a mist through the walls and the mosquito net. I got up, packed my stuff and marched up the muddy path. Lightning flashed and thunder rolled, and a candle glimmered on the second floor of the Swedes' house. In the chillout lounge I hung up my lantern and huddled in a hammock. "A perfect night to face the gargoyles," I thought. Tonight I would take 1.5 cups, which was as much as Sam, Scott and Ricardo put together.

One of Scott's sentinels came up the stairs with a flashlight and a rifle, and told me it was time for the ceremony. I packed up and followed him out the building and up the path. We walked through the trees and up to the foot of the ceremonial hall, looming in shadow at the top of the hill. There was neither candle- nor moonlight. Having brought me that far, the sentinel turned back to get the others and left me to enter the hall on my own. I went up the stairs and shined the light round the room to make sure I was alone. Then I went over to my pole and mechanically set up my things. Gradually the others trickled in. They settled into their places and turned off their lights, and together we waited in the dark. The insects buzzed in the trees, and occasionally a participant burped and spat into their bowl in nervous anticipation.

Eventually Scott and Ricardo came up the ramp, lit the candles and set up the ceremony. There were nine of us in total, and one by one we went up to receive our medicine. When it came my turn, Scott filled the cup to the rim. I put my lips to the liquid and drained it in two hard swallows. He took the cup back and refilled it half way, and I drank that too. I chased it with coffee and swilled my mouth out with water. Scott smiled at me as if to say "Easy now, you're in for quite a ride." I returned to my pole, spat bitter saliva into the bucket and closed my eyes.

Scott said a prayer and extinguished the candles. The liquid simmered in my gut, and with the darkness rose a hum in my ears and a strange pressure on my head and neck. I opened my eyes and saw the burning tip of Scott's cigarette drifting round the room. As it passed by, the air took on a lumpy texture like reptilian skin or frothy tar.

On its surface, disquieting little slits opened up and hissed at me with fine sharp teeth.

Ricardo broke into song and chased the hum out of my ears. The little mouths closed up and the lumpy pattern gave way to vibrant yellow and blue threads that undulated in the air like jellyfish tentacles. I was mesmerized by them, and barely noticed as Scott came over, took my head in his and hands and blew Agua Florida on it.

The threads had swayed like innocent décor at a safe distance, but suddenly they slowed to a halt and hung in the air like bars. I got the foreboding sense that the fun was over. They closed in and invaded my personal space, and all around me I heard excited whispers and impish giggles. I felt a frightening, alien presence, as if a wraith was putting its face up to mine. My body went numb and my heart pounded uncontrollably in my chest. I sat with my legs crossed and my back straight against the pole, and took long deep breaths. "Smile and remain detached," I told myself.

The intention of the thing to go inside me became as plain as my inability to hinder it. Rather than forcing its way in, however, it paused and paid me the courtesy to give it permission. I dared not resist. "Okay," I thought, "go for it," and it enveloped and entered me. It was like being possessed, and then the fireworks really started.

My body, the pole to my back and the bench to my bottom, the ceremonial hall and the jungle outside— all that anchored me in the physical world was torn away in one ferocious instant. It was like being yanked from one universe into another. I recall enormous crystalline jellyfish moving past me like moons in deep space, but most of the experience was too overwhelming to commit to memory. I was in sheer awe, and it was all I could do to keep breathing. I felt bliss and couldn't stop smiling, but Ayahuasca was no more personable or invested in me than the weather. It was an overwhelming force, and it tore through me like solar wind through tissue paper. It reached in, made me yawn like a puppet and made alterations so fine that my mind could only detect the iridescent pattern of their sum.

There was a dynamic to it. The energy coursed through me without hindrance as long as I remained a passive spectator. The moment that I cast a thought in words, however, fearful creatures strained toward me through the visions as if asking "Is there a human in our midst?!" Any further thought fueled their curiosity and gave them substance. I smiled, shook my head and cleared my mind, and they melted back into the pattern. I could only imagine the hell that Sam had gone through—soaked in sweat, retching for hours and whimpering in the corner—under the penetrating gaze of this devastating energy.

Again Scott came over, straddled my knee and blew floral water on my head, down my chest and along my arms. The body contact was comforting. He cradled my head, placed his hands over my heart and applied pressure to each knee and opposite shoulder. A coolness moved down my body.

I made fists, stretched until my frame shook and knew, for the first time, what my purpose was. I would tell the world about this! I would write a book, and remind people that their bodies are nothing more than vehicles and interfaces to this world. We operate within an illusion, a temporary dream, and mistake it for ourselves. This life is a fleeting story. We are not our name, culture, clothing, family, gender, age… not even our thoughts. We are that which perceives and gets caught up in these things, like the canvas on which a movie is projected.

This moment is a tooth on a cogwheel that revolves only once. You came from oblivion and will return to oblivion, and between those points you walk the Earth for a few years. Like a photon travels light-years from a star to your retina, my experience in the Amazon reaches you through these words. Notice how the details of your life fade into the background as you read this sentence, and yet you remain the same witnessing consciousness you have always been. That is who you were when you were born and who you will be when you die. Nothing will ever change that.

"Natalia will help you with this," the energy told me.

I yawned and took enormous breaths, and a bitter gurgling started up in my stomach. No sooner had I reached for the bowl than my innards contracted and pushed their contents out through my mouth. Everyone in the room heard me, but I didn't care. Again and again I retched from the deepest corners of my gut. I gasped and panted into the bowl. My face was wet with sweat and tears, but I felt great. My insides were lean and the bitterness had subsided. I felt reborn, and my Vancouver existence seemed a lifetime away.

Gradually the effects faded, and at midnight the sentinels fired their rifles. Scott sent the spirits away with a prayer and lit the candles. Slowly life returned to the group. Many had vomited. I stood up to meet Scott as he came over to check on me, and gave him a long hug.

"Thank you," I told him.

"How'd it go?" he asked.

"It was wonderful," I said. "It'll take me time to make sense of it." Scott patted my shoulder and seemed pleased.

Ricardo came over as well, spoke to me in Spanish and smiled. "Thank you!" I said, and gave the little man a warm hug. He was awkward with it and squirmed a little. I wondered if I'd breached some kind of rule about touching the shaman, but I didn't care. My energy was good and my appreciation was genuine; how could anyone object to that?

I went across the room to where Sam sat in quiet contemplation. He was relieved that my trip had gone well. From the sound of my purge, he had thought that I was in trouble.

Sam's ceremony had been a breakthrough much like my own, although his descriptions were more animated than mine. He said that an eagle had appeared and pecked bad energy from his lung, and a lion had wrapped a long wide tail around him. He had seen his mother and beamed love and energy into her chest, but her damage writhed around her like a black octopus and resisted the healing.

We packed up and left the hall. Sam and I walked together while the others went ahead. It was still raining, but the canopy caught most of it. We stopped for a glass of lemonade at the main building and then marched on with our lights trained on our boots.

It was remarkable how the ceremony had seeded goals and provided direction. I knew that I would quit my job and write a book, and Sam wanted to become a shaman. We talked about how our mothers, who were tragic figures in both our lives, might profit from such an experience. We realized however that that would never happen, nor was it necessary. Ayahuasca was not a cure-all. Each of us faced their challenges in their own time and in their own way.

At some point we stopped, looked around and felt lost. The path had disappeared among the leaves, the mud and the lingering visions. We tracked back and realized that we'd walked past Sam's house without noticing. Sam invited me up for a smoke but I declined, although I regretted passing up the bonding opportunity. I wanted to keep a clear head and get home to record my thoughts. The large Arab gave me a long bear hug, wished me a good night and went into his house.

I walked home, went upstairs and lit a candle. The wick sizzled with moisture. I took off the boots and placed them side by side on the floor, bracing the top of one against the other to keep it from folding over. I draped a damp towel over my shoulders to block the mosquitoes, pulled out my diary and began to write.

Fire and brimstone

The world was an image on a movie screen and Ayahuasca was the door to the projection booth. I couldn't believe that such a thing was possible! I had woken up to a new universe—to a whole new state of being—and couldn't wait for the next ceremony.

The following day flew by with its meals, chillouts and requisite nap, and in the evening Sam and I were the first to go to the ceremonial hall. Sam sat on the bench and meditated, and I lay on the ground on my inflatable mattress. When Scott and the rest of the crew arrived, I placed my hand on the floor to push myself up and crushed a large cockroach. I flicked the carcass under the bench and hoped that no one had noticed, but that failed to prevent it from foreshadowing the tone of the upcoming ceremony.

I took 1.5 cups, same as the previous night, and felt nauseous almost immediately. I returned to my seat and the altered state come on even before the candles were extinguished. As I sat against the pole and watched the proceedings, a rumble like that of construction machinery rose in my ears. Everything vibrated, and I was mercilessly pulled into a tunnel the likes of which one might traverse on the way to hell. The walls were jagged stone and illuminated as if by fire.

Things did not going well. Scott didn't come around and the shaman threw up. Without guidance, the experience threatened to get out of control. I strained for composure and hyperventilated as the frantically racing visions shook me like a dog shakes a toy. A large insect landed on the back of my hand and gripped the entire surface with it's barbed legs. I gave it a frantic shake and felt its weight as it peeled off.

It took over an hour for Ricardo to break into song and when he did, it failed to provide the solace I had hoped. His chant was forlorn and heavy, and sounded in places like despairing gasps. It was heartrending. I was cocooned in something like a brown leaf or a dead pea pod, and fierce lights strobed red and yellow on the membrane's surface. I held the bowl in my lap and yawned into it, feeling that I would throw up any moment, but relief wouldn't come. I wanted nothing more than to get the stuff out of me.

Across the room I heard Sam throw up and was thankful that I wasn't suffering alone. I smiled with tears in my eyes and told myself: "I can do this! I can deal with whatever happens!" A second insect landed on my cheek and fluttered under my hand as I brushed it away.

"Do what you have to do!" I told it. "Reach in as deep as you need and fix whatever you need to fix! Thank you! Thank you for forcing me to take responsibility!"

Two hours into the ceremony I finally threw up. The spasms were painful and I continued to dry heave after the liquid was gone. Scott appeared out of nowhere, took the bowl from my hands and emptied it over the railing. "How are you doing?" he asked.

"It's harder this time," I whispered. "I almost freaked out."

Scott took a swig and began blowing Agua Florida on my head, when Ricardo made a mistake in his chant and sent me giggling like a schoolboy in church. Scott started laughing too and almost choked on the cologne. He gave my shoulder a squeeze and continued on his way. From then on the evening was fairly pleasant.

After the rifles fired and the candles were lit, I went over to Sam. I patted him on the back and sat down next to him. "How'd it go?" I asked cheerfully. "You know, whenever you get sick it brings a smile to my face!"

Sam's gaze remained fixed on the floor. "I don't want to talk about it," he said, and then I knew that I had crossed a line. I sat beside him in awkward silence, daring neither to leave nor speak. He grabbed his stuff and disappeared down the ramp.

The rest of us left as a group and stepped out of the covered staircase into a crystal clear night. The stars twinkled in the heavens and a single wisp of cloud mysteriously veiled the moon. I noticed that Mikael was disoriented and hung back to see that he was alright. He staggered up to a tree, braced himself against it and threw up. The other Swedes came back and looked after him.

I marched ahead and caught up with Scott. We walked up to the main building and waited for the others by the lemonade table.

"You're becoming quite a psychonaut," he commented, "and you're learning quickly. You handled yourself well through that rough patch tonight, especially with the high dose you're taking. I guess that's what it takes to push you around."

He walked me home, came upstairs, lit a candle and grabbed a seat. He looked like a wise gnome with his white hair and beard, and twinkling black eyes. The air around him danced with colored static.

"The effects are still quite strong," I told him. "I hope the clowns don't come."

"I don't think you need to worry," he said, "there shouldn't be any more teeth tonight. This house is built in a corner of the forest that has particularly good energy. Tonight the insects will be your teachers."

What are we doing?!

At night we enter a round room, drink horribly bitter liquid and sit with our backs against poles like psychedelic Borg connecting to the collective through wooden alcoves, or like Odysseus when he tied himself to the mast and listened to the Siren's song. For four hours we step through a door and surrender ourselves to a mysterious energy.

Scott described it as follows:

> "It's a wild walk in another dimension. You say 'My God, I'm finally alive!' There is the danger of taking on a negative picture, so it's important not to clutch. It's important to be your own advocate.

Come to peace with your own energy field, both the good and the bad side; everything is a part of you and you don't have to make apologies. If you don't create your world someone else will create it for you, and that's not what you need."

The hell session

I woke up feeling thin and weak after having regurgitated the Refugio's light diet for the second night in a row. On shaky legs I walked to the main building and joined the others for breakfast. The omelet, buns and coffee made me feel better.

I felt like something was changing in me. Not my thoughts or my views, but the emotional core of me. It was as if a rickety structure of willy-nilly nailed together boards was slowly melting into a shiny golden ball. I mentioned this to Scott. "What happens to us in the ceremony?" I asked. "I feel like I'm being reprogrammed."

"That impression is a valid one," replied Scott. "The medicine builds a conduit in your nervous system which in future can be activated without the use of sacred tools. It's a line that runs from your conscious to your subconscious, and beyond to the collective and non-human worlds. Everyone perceives this in their own way. Christians call it love, Buddhists call it detachment and Hindus call it ecstasy or Krishna. You are on your way to becoming fully mature. It brings with it a spontaneity and freedom to do what is needed. Most adults just play the part without really being grown up. They buy into a routine and stop growing."

We topped up our coffees and went to the hammock lounge. Scott pointed over the railing to a small hut at the edge of the field where something was burning. "We're making a fresh batch of medicine," he said.

"How do you make it?" I asked.

"We cut up Chacruna and Ayahuasca and boil them together for 12 hours. Ayahuasca is a vine and Chacruna a shrub, and neither is psychoactive on it's own. From two large cauldrons we get about eight bottles of medicine."

"How did people ever figure out to combine two innocuous plants, from the thousands that grow in the Amazon, to such profound effect?"

"According to legend, when the Indians came to this world their parents gave them Ayahuasca and told them to plant it wherever they go. It's easy: you bury a branch, put some leaves over top and it sprouts and grows. In three years you can harvest it. Ayahuasca is used by all tribes and it's presence usually indicates human activity. The tribes are nomadic. They move from one hunting ground to the next and the jungle eats up all man-made structures, but the Ayahuasca remains."

"When are you going to use this batch?" I asked.

"Tonight. The medicine is best when it's fresh; it tastes almost like tea. The bitterness develops as it ferments in the bottle."

"I'd like to try it, but I feel weak from the past two nights."

"Give it some thought. Tomorrow we'll take a break, so you can definitely rest then."

I walked out to the hut to check out the Ayahuasca production. The hut consisted of four posts and a conical roof. In the middle of the floor lay two concrete beams, side by side, and between them burned a fire. Two enormous pots–large enough for me to sit in–straddled the beams, and from their mouths rose so much steam that their contents were obscured. I stared into the hypnotic billows and thought about how many pots had boiled like this throughout history, and how many visions they had unleashed.

"Of course I will attend the ceremony," I thought. "That's why I'm here." I returned to the chillout lounge and dozed in a hammock until dinner. After dinner I walked to my house and went to bed.

I woke up after a few hours, looked around the darkness and saw a light through the wall, coming toward me down the path. When it came close I heard Sam's voice call out "Can I come up?!"

"Sure," I called back, "as long as you don't mind me in my skibbies!" I put on my head light and sat cross-legged on the bed. Sam came up the stairs. "Grab a seat," I said. "Is it time for the ceremony?"

"No, not yet," he said. Sam was out of breath and appeared nervous. "Don't take this personally," he continued. "This is a recurring issue for me and I have the same problem with my girlfriend. I let people in too much.

I need you to keep your distance in the ceremony tonight, and in general."

"Sure," I said.

"Cool," he replied. He turned around, climbed down the stairs and left the house. A shadow passed over my heart. I sat in silence and watched the light disappear into the jungle.

I got myself ready and walked to the ceremonial hall with measured steps. Sam was already there. I inflated the mattress, tucked my pants into my socks and applied mosquito repellent. Everyone arrived and settle into there places.

Before commencing the ceremony, Scott announced: "We made a fresh batch of medicine today. We cooked it an hour longer than usual, so it may be a little stronger." One by one he called us up.

"Otto," he said.

I walked up and sat beside him in the flickering light. "What do you think?" I asked. "Should I maybe take one cup instead of one and a half? Last night was fairly intense and you said this batch is even stronger."

"I wouldn't worry about it," he replied, "you might as well go whole hog. Tomorrow we'll all take a day off." He poured the medicine and I gulped it down. Not only did it taste nothing like tea, but it was so harsh that it scorched my throat.

The hum began in my ears as I crossed the room back to my seat. Whatever comprised the barrier between me and the altered state—be it urban distractions, scientific theories or beef in my diet—it had worn alarmingly thin. It took but a nudge to push me through. I sat bolt upright with my face limp, eyes closed and mouth open; like an android awaiting its programming.

Scott said a prayer, extinguished the candles and came around with Agua Florida and tobacco smoke.

Ricardo began his song, and conjured fiery threads in the air. I wondered what the others saw and imagined someone walking into the hall, someone with the ability to perceive other people's hallucinations, and seeing us in columns of luminescent phantasmagoria like in strange spiritual display cases.

The more I stared into the threads the more detail appeared on them. Like lava that heated up with my attention, their surfaces crackled and revealed ever brighter colors within. In no time they whittled down to their piercing white cores and before I knew what was happening, I was back in the strobing clown world I had visited on the bathroom floor after the first ceremony. The infernal tykes flooded into me and this time they were accompanied by a heinous over-clown who orchestrated the proceedings. He appeared to me in frightful guises, but that struck me as a diversion or a cruel game, and not his main intent. His actual purpose was to disarm and burn his crystalline strobe light, layer after layer, into the deepest parts of me.

Never before had I known such agony! I reached for the bowl, placed it in my lap and tried in vain to purge the liquid. My heart pounded in my face and I grew damp in a flash of sweat. I slumped over the bowl and gasped and panted into it. The acid seethed in my gut and crawled up my throat. I winced and tried to smile, and whispered "Thank you, thank you..." over and over. It was all I could do.

At long last, after an hour of this, I threw up. Again and again I screamed into the bowl. My guts cramped inside out. Scott came over, emptied the bowl and returned it to my lap. "Breathe..." he said.

I expected the experience to mellow out after that, now that the Ayahuasca had been expelled, but it didn't. My mind was devoured in a blinding white scream, my body twitched and my hand involuntarily flung the bowl across the floor with a bang. I fumbled in the dark and retrieved it.

Suddenly it occurred to me that I might be damaged by this. "What if I never come down?" I thought. "What if I become schizophrenic and permanently lose my grip on reality?!" At that moment the maniacal clown reared up and howled with laughter, his face twisted into infinite images like in a demonic hall of mirrors. He reached his snaky fingers into me, burrowed them through me like worms and shouted "DO YOU WANT TO SEE ME BREAK IT?! DO YOU?!!!"

"No!" I gasped. "Please don't! Please!" I had visions of me curled into a ball and rocking in the corner of an asylum with a broken mind.

It continued like that for the remaining hours, and I purged two more times. Slowly-slowly the intensity waned. Scott did what he could, brought water and blew Agua Florida, but it was of little use. I realized that no one controlled this. Scott and Ricardo were facilitators and gatekeepers, and the rest of us were children stepping naked and alone into an abyss where nothing from this world could reach us.

The rifles sounded at midnight. Scott uttered a prayer and clicked his lighter, and candlelight flickered on my eyelids. I opened my eyes and had trouble connecting with the room. Sounds echoed in my ears and objects smudged in my visual field. People got up, walked around and whispered to each other. I remained seated for a long time.

The others began leaving as I crawled off the bench onto my hands and knees and began rolling up the mattress. It was exhausting. When I was done Scott was the only one left. I apologized for taking so long and stumbled after him into the night.

"You made some intense progress tonight," he said.

"It doesn't feel that way," I replied.

He walked me home and lit a candle on my table. "Have a good night," he said, and left.

I got myself ready and climbed into bed. The Ayahuasca still burned in my throat. I closed my eyes and saw vivid images of grotesquely deformed faces. They bubbled with goiter-like swellings and insect bristles welled from their eye sockets. I tossed and turned, and tried to get them out of my mind.

Suddenly everything fell silent and I found myself in an enormous dark space with a single object in the far corner. It was a brown pod of a material like the chitinous exoskeleton of a cockroach, and it glowed yellow from within. It was a cross between an insect cocoon and a plant bud. I approached it with apprehension and studied the beautiful texture on its glowing surface. I reached out and touched it, and it opened up into something like an escape pod. There was a comfortable room inside with soft lighting, soothing music and a plush bench round its perimeter. I climbed in and the pod closed up.

As if a record had skipped, I was back where I started: in the dark room with the pod in the corner. This time I approached it with more confidence. When I touched it, a monstrous jack-in-the-box burst out and towered over me. It roared with hideous laughter, rained crystals and knives down on me and shouted: "DO YOU WANT TO DIE NOW?!"

"No!" I pleaded. "I want to return to the human world and live an ordered life!"

The seventh day

I lay on my back, stared into the mosquito net and listened to the rain that began at dawn. "My body is in the Amazon," I thought, "and every night we drink strange stuff, trip out and throw up, and every day we store up energy to do it all over again. What a surreal and self indulgent loop! How can I return to society and deal with its games after this?"

77

I sat up, parted the net and looked around the room. The floor was larger than my apartment in Vancouver. The air was fresh and an ocean of plants toward up around the building. This was how humans were meant to live: in nature and in a warm climate, true to their inborn rhythms and drives.

I showered and shaved, got dressed and walked to the main building. "Good morning," I said as I came up the stairs. Scott, Sam and the Swedes were having breakfast.

"Good morning," replied Scott. "How was your night?"

I sat down and took a deep breath. "I feel like crap," I said. "I got little sleep and saw ghastly things all night. I realized that Ayahuasca is like insect consciousness: it's alien, it's fragmented like compound eyes and it invades your nervous system like so many bugs. It even sounds like insects as it comes on."

"You want to keep your mind and body strong," said Scott. "The path is balance. After three days of one and a half cups your system is saturated with medicine. Eat, exercise and get plenty R&R and social contact. That's very important. You don't want to sacrifice anything. As for the insects, they are powerful allies and excellent survival machines, but they are only one of many spirits. Other people think it's a realm of gnomes, dwarfs, fairies and angels."

"And clowns," I added bitterly. "How do you deal with it? How are you able to walk around and function while the rest of us are freaking out?"

"It comes with the profession," he said, "just as a surgeon doesn't pass out at the sight of blood. As your perspective expands you see that the good contains the bad and the bad contains the good, and in the end its all the same thing."

I reached for the juice pitcher, strained to lift it and poured myself a glass. Someone set a plate with chicken omelet in front me. It seemed like a lot, but I chewed through it conscientiously while the others talked. My body absorbed the nutriment like a sponge. My back straightened and my shoulders relaxed.

All of a sudden I imagined Sam, sitting obliviously next to me, grabbing my diary, hurling it over the railing into the rain and reducing my precious thoughts and stories to a muddy pulp. I imagined catching his hand as he reached for it, twisting it round and breaking his elbow. My hands grew hot as I played it over and over in my mind. Trying to look nonchalant I took the diary, sealed it in the zip-lock bag and returned it to my pack. I stared into space and let the anger wash through me.

A woman brought a thermos of fresh coffee and our eyes met as she set it down on the table. We exchanged a smile, and with that my aggression changed to sexual arousal. It was intense. I imagined following her downstairs, embracing her and pressing my erect penis against her body.

I poured myself a coffee and retreated to a hammock in the chillout lounge. As I closed my eyes, I sank headfirst through the material into a black void. The familiar hum from the ceremony rang in my ears, and a cloud of sparkling creatures swarmed around me. Wherever they touched me I felt soothed and nourished.

A pixie, no bigger than my palm, appeared out of nowhere. Although proportioned like a dainty diminutive human, it was a far cry from Tinker Bell. It's skin was segmented plates of green-gray armor like an insect's, it's eyes were like polished orbs of emerald crystal and its wings were like a dragonfly's. It zipped around excitedly and popped into my belly. I felt it move up my spine, up my neck and into my skull, and then it burst from the top of my head with a poof of glittering dust. It came around, hovered in front of my face and studied me with its luminous eyes. Then it swooped in, gave me a kiss and flew away.

Slowly I opened my eyes. The rain had stopped and residual water dripped from the eaves. It felt as if the little pixie had been with me all along, watching over me since I arrived at the Refugio. Maybe it had been with me and orchestrating events all my life. Maybe the clowns in the ceremony were the pixie in disguise, and maybe everything—including the pixie, my thoughts and the entire world—was countless projections of a single thing.

I struggled to my feet, walked to the dining room to get more coffee and noticed the British couple sitting at a table in the far corner. I poured the coffee, added sugar and condensed milk, and went over to them while stirring the cup.

"May I join you?" I asked cautiously. "I think I just saw a fairy."

Their faces lit up. "See?" said the man, and pulled out a chair for me. "Please."

I sat down and told them about the insectoid pixie with the emerald eyes. "I don't expect it to exist for anyone but me," I added at the end, "but whatever it was, I saw a fairy."

"Oh, don't worry about that," replied the man. "You cannot be objective about something that is subjective. We are guided by our emotions and the mind only interprets will into it. What's important is that you saw it."

"It's like a ring," said the woman. "There is no path to follow and no place to enter into it. Something has to kick you there."

A pale mist rolled into the jungle and the rain returned with a thunderstorm. The water hit the roof so hard that we had to yell to be heard. We took an early supper and then retired to our houses.

I tried reading a book in the hammock on my porch, but the light was dim and the rope that held the candle lantern cast a shadow that rocked back and forth across the page. I dropped the book in my lap, closed my eyes and listened to the weather. I felt lonely. I had no one to talk to and nothing to do, and wished I could hug Natalia, my mother and my friends. I wished I were home.

I went to bed early, curled into a ball and shivered under the clammy sheet. Thunder crackled in the distance. I closed my eyes, sank into sleep and emerged in a sunny glade, sitting with my back against a tree. Butterflies and pollen danced in the air and the sky swirled with joyous colors. Everything was wonderful except the bitter taste of Ayahuasca rising in my stomach. I swallowed to keep it down, and with that the image dissolved and I found myself back in bed with the storm raging outside.

The final ceremony

The following morning I found a little white ball on the floor next to the stairs. I leaned down to get a better look, and saw that it was a dead honey bee blanketed in mold. I scooped it to the side so that I wouldn't step on it. After getting ready I reached for my nylon backpack and discovered a dense crop of miniature alfalfa sprouting from its side. I realized that the jungle flora would consume you as surely as any animal.

"It's been over 24 hours since the last ceremony," I told Scott at breakfast, "and I still feel out of it. How long is this going to last?"

"You'll feel better soon," he said, "but you have made a bid to expand your awareness. You have invited a world of extremely complex energies and this cuts both ways; you see them and they see you. It'll keep you on your toes."

"Are you saying that I'm going to see ghosts from now on?" I asked.

"The spirits are tricksters," he replied, "and will mess with you any way they can. For example, the other day I was walking home after a ceremony when I tripped on something and fell flat on my face. My flashlight hit the ground, blew open and the batteries launched into the jungle. At the same time, something shrieked "GACK-GACK-GACK-GACK!" from behind a tree. I picked myself up, used my lighter to gather the components, reassembled the flashlight and got the hell out of there. When I got home and closed the door behind me, a thin voice called "hhheeelp meee, hhheeelp meee" from the jungle. I thought that someone might be in trouble and strained to listen, and then the voice came louder: "HHHEEELP MEEE!" For a moment I considered going out to investigate, but then decided it was probably a trick. If someone really was out there, they could wait till morning. The voice stopped after that.

"The spirits teach us to smile at ghouls, to remain calm no matter what happens and to act rather than react. With this attitude you can weather anything the physical world throws at you. It's all about balance."

Once again I was struck by the profoundly strange and challenging path that Scott had chosen for himself. He took Ayahuasca about four times a week and had done so for years. His mind straddled a hairline between two worlds. I feared the Pandora's box I had opened and that lunatic clowns would reach for me from the shadows for the rest of my life.

"Maybe I should stop while I'm ahead," I said. "I don't know if I can take any more."

"You should get back on the horse," replied Scott simply. "You could reduce it to one cup."

"No way," I said, "no more than half."

The day flew by and before I knew it, Scott's sentinel called to me from the front of my house. It was the first time that they had to get me out of bed. I was frightened, but I knew that Scott was right. If I didn't stand up to this I would live in fear for the rest of my life.

We hiked to the ceremonial hall and I settled into my corner. I breathed deeply and watched nervously as Scott called the others up.

"Otto."

I went up and sat beside him. "So," he whispered. "One cup?"

"Half a cup," I replied firmly. "I'm not doing any more." I did not mean to be cowardly or disappoint Scott, but it was my mind that was on the line. Besides, half a cup was nothing to scoff at. I drank the Ayahuasca and returned to my seat. Scott said a prayer, extinguished the candles and walked around with the Agua Florida and tobacco smoke.

The caustic liquid pooled dark and creamy in my gut, and effervesced with rainbow colored circles, squares and triangles. The hum rose in my ears and the threads wavered into view, and immediately the dark haze that had hung over me since the last ceremony lifted. I was back! Like a ray of sunshine through the clouds, my quirky, cocky and adventurous personality returned to me.

I saw the patterns and felt the clowns, but they could not force themselves on me as before. This was certainly because I had taken less medicine, but I had also figured out how they operated. Like a hypnotist telling you that you're walking down a staircase and getting sleepier with each step, they coaxed you into, through or down something. A fractal pattern would bloom open and pull you into it's center with intriguing textures and vibrant colors. As you relaxed and gave it your attention, you dropped your guard and let them in.

I would have welcomed the spirits had they been agreeable guests–after all, I had traveled to the Amazon to meet them–but they seemed to disregard me entirely. Their aim was to dig beneath my personality, deep into the marrow of my mind, and strobe it with painfully bright light. Had they been monsters I might have understood them, but these things had a twisted intelligence about them; a cloying crystalline insanity like sentient toys in a dead boy's room.

As I sat against the pole and held the visions at bay I felt a stick, no thicker than my finger, poke firmly into my cheek. I imagined a tree stooping down, looking into the hall and curiously reaching in a branch. Perhaps it was an insect or an illusion but whatever it was, I did nothing. After a while it pulled away and disappeared.

I felt that I had mastered the situation. I stood up, placed the mattress on the floor and lay down with my limbs spreadeagled from me. The clowns rampaged behind the images like dogs snarling against a car window, and tried to force their way through. "Fuck you!" I screamed in my mind. "You fucking clowns!!! Did you think I'd let you in after what you did to me?!"

Suddenly a thumping sound reached through the hallucinatory fog and shook the floor. I wondered if I was in danger; maybe an animal had entered the hall, or an angry man. I didn't have much time to consider it, however, because a foot stomped on my face, stomach and hand, and a body crashed into the bench beside me. I caught the person around the waist as they fell to the floor and recognized Camilla, the Swedish girl.

"What are you doing?!" I hissed.

She mumbled incoherently and then fell silent.

"Hey!" I whispered angrily, and gave her a shake. "Are you okay? What are you doing?!"

She gasped sharply as if I'd startled her from sleep. "What?!" she exclaimed. "Oh, I'm going to the bathroom."

"Why did you run blindly across the room?! Why didn't you use your flashlight?"

"I thought I knew the way." Her body relaxed and she turned around and gave me a hug. "Sorry," she said, and returned to her seat.

I sat cross legged on the mattress, collected my thoughts and checked my body for injuries. There was no wetness so I assumed I wasn't bleeding.

Scott came over. "What happened?" he whispered.

"Camilla ran across the room and stomped on me," I said. "She said she was on her way to the bathroom, but that doesn't make much sense."

"That's why I like to take people there myself," he chided. "Are you alright?"

"My hand's a bit numb, but I'm fine."

"Okay," he said, and went to check on Camilla.

I massaged my hand and discovered that the tip of my little finger was oddly loose. I could flex it to make a fist, but it hung limp when I extended it. Since I felt no pain I assumed that a nerve had been damaged.

I lay down and closed my eyes, and the clowns made no noteworthy appearance for the rest of the ceremony. After the rifles fired and the candles were lit, I packed up and walked home with Scott.

"Ever since I arrived," I told him, "I've been trying to make sense of all this. Please tell me if I understand this correctly: the physical world is a projection of the spirit world or, the other way around, the spiritual is a rarefied version of the physical. Either way, the too are intimately connected."

"Yes," he agreed.

"Now, Ayahuasca, which is at the same time a psychoactive drug and a spirit, takes us to the spirit world and mediates our interaction with it. Paradoxically, although we all go to the same place, we find the spiritual dimension not outside of ourselves like a tree in a field, but rather in the depths of our own minds."

"That's right."

"So, if we're all in the same place, does that mean that a given spirit has access to all who engage in the ceremony?"

"Yes."

"And if someone was to anger a spirit, would it be possible for that spirit to possess another participant in the ceremony and use their body to avenge itself?"

"Absolutely."

"Do you think that's what happened tonight?"

"It's entirely possible, but that's not a fruitful line of inquiry. Important is only what you learn from it."

What if the clowns had actually possessed Camilla? That would mean that all this stuff was real! It was one thing to see images in your mind's eye and have your sensory data distorted, but quite another to have those visions reach into this world and hurt you. My faith in a division between my thoughts and the physical world dissolved.

Scott brought me home, lit a candle and left. I went downstairs and avoided looking in the mirror as I brushed my teeth. "Even if the spirits are real," I thought, "it seems that they can only reach into this world through other creatures, and only then if those creatures are amenable to it. Drugs, fatigue and emotions are gateways for them to connect to us, so that means I'm wide open."

I returned upstairs, sat on the bed and wrote anything in my diary to keep my eyes open and the nib moving across the page. The ink ran out and I replaced the cartridge. As I expounded on the differences between the effects of Ayahuasca and magic mushrooms, a fatigue so leaden took hold of me that I assumed the spirits were pulling me into unconsciousness. My eyes sagged, my head bobbed and my writing telescoped until I scribbled on a single spot.

When I could resist no longer, I got up and fetched a windup flashlight which my mother had given me on my trip. I put away the diary and the headlight, lay on my back and wound the dynamo. The object in my hands was a reminder that my mother loved me, and its whirring sound anchored me in the physical world when the light of my eyes could not. Like a magic jewel, it chased the shadows from my bed, my thoughts and my heart.

Behind my closed eyes appeared a set of double doors made of heavy wood. After a moment, they swung open into a luxurious Christmas room in an English parlor. A hearty fire crackled in the fireplace and candles glowed on the branches of the Christmas tree. All around the room, cheerful toys played as if they were alive. A doll rode a rocking horse, toy soldiers marched about, maracas shook themselves in the air and a teddy bear and a nutcracker warmed themselves by the fire.

I moved closer and was about to step over the threshold, when I noticed that all the toys were red and white like the face paint of a clown. Alarmed that the spirits were trying to lure me in, I froze in mid step. The joyful activity ground to a halt and in unison the toys turned their heads to look at me. Only now did I recognize the malevolent expressions painted on their faces. The doors swung shut and left me in the dark.

I wound the flashlight in my hands and the light grew brighter. In my dream, the wooden panels of the corridor came into view. I turned to my left and saw that the light came from a staircase at the end of the hall. I moved toward it, and with each step I drifted deeper into pillowy sleep until I realized that the staircase led down into the floor and the light shining from its bottom was red. Again I stopped, and immediately the light shut off.

It continued like that all night long.

A new horizon

If we believe in something that does not exist, it will have a weak reality in our minds. If we believe in something that does exist, then we will draw that thing into our lives. Either way, whatever we pay attention to becomes real. It becomes real for us, and that is the only reality we can ever know.

From the moment we are born, we are subjected to enormous amounts of mind control. Individuals and organizations seek to impress their views upon us, and many go through life defending thoughts and beliefs that were never their own.

The most important aspect of shamanism is that it changes your paradigm. The spirit world is an emotional training ground, and every experience teaches us something. We can move forward only when we accept things for what they are and focus on solutions rather than problems.

Return to civilization

My time at the Refugio drew to a close, and one by one the visitors left. First the Swedes, then me and finally Sam. The British family likely stayed until their money ran out, or until the father either died or convalesced; whichever came first.

My finger showed no sign of improvement. The flaccid tip caught in my sleeves and in my pockets, but it was a small price to pay for one of the most impelling experiences of my life. It could have ended much, much worse.

On the morning of my departure I packed my things, took a last heavy-hearted look around the house and walked up the hill to Scott's place to return his boots. Scott invited me up, and I seized the opportunity to photograph three of his paintings. The paintings were by different artists, and yet remarkably similar interpretations of the Ayahuasca experience. In the center of each canvas was an enclosed space—a circle or a hut—in which a shaman administered Ayahuasca to someone. The rest of the canvas was filled with a swirling ocean of spirit creatures. The idea was that our world is a bubble within a greater realm, like a campfire in a forest.

"So," I said, "those are the creatures that will try to manipulate me."

"Whatever happens," said Scott, "remain calm. You're very open right now and the spirits will challenge you on the rest of your journey. The door will close with time, especially if you eat red meat and change your views. A mind cannot see what it cannot accept. Now, we must get going. Email me any questions you have and I'll be happy to answer them."

We left the house and walked along the path to the stairs I had come up, exhausted and dehydrated, ten days before. Much had happened since then. We climbed down the stairs and into a boat where Jose was waiting for us, and pulled into the peaceful backwaters of the Amazon. I stared into the opaque water as it streamed by, and imagined ancient cities concealed in its depths.

We merged into a larger river and chased down a water taxi, and transferred me on the open water. Scott paid for my ticket, gave me a hug and told me to keep in touch. Jose turned the boat around and they headed back to the Refugio.

The water taxi was packed. I squeezed onto the front bench between a fat woman cradling a child and a muscular young man in a tank top, and guarded my belongings between my feet. The man nodded at the staff in my hand and commented: "Un pitón!"

"Hmm-hmm, si," I agreed.

I had purchased the walking stick, carved like snake, from a native women on the platform in front of the main building. Scott had haggled a good price for me, and commented that it was a "nice piece" and a "real power staff". Next to my diary, it was my most prized possession. It made me feel safe, as if it created a protective barrier around me.

Scott's warning rang in my ears and I thought: "I'll deal with whatever happens. The clowns no longer have a hold on me." Just then, the speedboat hit a log with a frightful bang. The man on look-out laughed nervously and stole a glance back at the driver. The fat woman slapped him on the thigh and scolded him in Spanish. I closed my eyes, felt the staff in my hands and cleared my mind.

In Iquitos I took a rickshaw to the guest house where the Swedes were staying. After checking in, I walked past the reception into a long atrium. The floor was tiled, the roof was open to the sky and lawn chairs and potted plants lined the sides. At the far end, I found the Swedes preparing Glögg—a hot Christmas drink with red wine, fruits, nuts and spices—in a small kitchen area.

They handed me a cup and invited me to their room where incense curled in the air, candles glowed and chillout music played on an mp3 player with portable speakers. A guitar leaned in the corner, and my mind flashed to my damaged finger. Camilla had never raised the subject or asked how I was doing, although she knew that she had injured me. I considered broaching the topic with her, but then thought better of it. What was the point? At best she would tell me again that she was sorry and that she had been on her way to the bathroom. I doubted that she had any further insight into her actions.

On the floor stood a padded display board with necklaces and earrings pinned to it. Mikael explained that a drug dealer had left it with them while he went to fetch his stash. The dealer soon returned, looking like a holy man. He was tall and dark skinned with a flowing black beard and a clean white robe. On his head he wore an outrageous cylinder of a hat woven of wide strips of leaf. It looked like a waste basket. He was polite and poised, had a twinkle in his eye and brought a pleasant energy into the room. He greeted me with a handshake, sat down, rolled a joint and passed it around.

As the Swedes and the dealer bargained, I leaned back and watched Disney's animated version of Alice in Wonderland playing on the muted TV. "How apropos," I thought. The joint came around a few more times and the conversation meandered to the nature of life and reality. I pulled out my diary and recorded the following snippets:

"People buy clothes and make-up and bullshit technology when all they miss is their soul."

"Maybe it's just a big loop. We keep going and going and keep making decisions. I like living."

"The future lies ahead of us and we have filters in the way—a car, a house, a job—but if you take those away it's just life."

"The Shipibo say that we should look at the world through Ayahuasca, and not through television."

Epilogue

I returned to Vancouver and spent two years writing this book, and Natalia helped me along the way. Should I ever doubt my own story, I have my little finger to remind me.

Thank you.

About the Author

Born in Germany and raised in Canada, Otto Matthias grew up between both European and North American cultures. This led him to identify not with any one language or nationality, but to recognize their relativity and the folly of seeking oneself in such attributes. When he was nineteen, Otto had a mystical experience – a glimpse of cosmic consciousness – that affirmed for him that the world is a fleeting form and a narrative to test our spirit.

Although Otto spent many years in formal education and attained degrees in Psychology and Business Management, his intellectual mainspring has been his insatiable curiosity. He forever seeks a greater understanding of reality, and uses whatever means available to explore his mind and travel the world. Through years of sharing his thoughts and impressions, he has honed his craft and sought to liberate people from the illusory bonds of daily strife.

When the Fire goes out is Otto's first book, and a personal triumph. Through the act of writing it, he has faced his fears and discovered that the world reflects to us our own beliefs.